THE
FATEFUL
TRIANGLE

Race, Ethnicity, Nation

STUART HALL

Edited by
Kobena Mercer

———

Foreword by
Henry Louis Gates, Jr.

HARVARD UNIVERSITY PRESS
Cambridge, Massachusetts, and London, England
2017

Library of Congress Cataloging-in-Publication Data

Names: Hall, Stuart, 1932–2014, author.
Title: The fateful triangle : race, ethnicity, nation / Stuart Hall ;
edited by Kobena Mercer, with a foreword by
Henry Louis Gates, Jr.
Description: Cambridge, Massachusetts : Harvard University Press,
2017. | Includes bibliographical references and index.
Identifiers: LCCN 2017006478 | ISBN 9780674976528 (alk. paper)
Subjects: LCSH: Ethnicity. | Race—Political aspects. |
Ethnocentrism. | Nation-state and globalization.
Classification: LCC GN495.6 .H34 2017 | DDC 305.8—dc23
LC record available at https://lccn.loc.gov/2017006478

for Becky and Jess

CONTENTS

FOREWORD

Henry Louis Gates, Jr.

> When Europeans of the Old World first encoun-
> tered the peoples and cultures of the New
> World in the 1400s, they put to themselves a
> great question: not "Are you not a son and a
> brother, are you not a daughter and a sister?" . . .
> but rather: "Are these true men? Do they belong
> to the same species as us? Or are they born of
> another creation?"
>
> —STUART HALL (Du Bois Lectures, Lecture 1)

STUART HALL didn't come to Harvard University
to give the Du Bois Lectures in April 1994 to reinforce
what we already knew. And he wasn't interested in re-
hashing old arguments or adding to the chorus of
scholars who, for decades, had valiantly exposed
"race" as a social construct, a linguistic phenomenon

having little to do with biology and everything to do with power. Hall had already seen beyond this view; in a world hurtling toward globalization, what fascinated him were the centrality and stubborn endurance of "race" as a marker of essential biological differences, despite the best efforts of so many brilliant minds, at least from W. E. B. Du Bois to Kwame Anthony Appiah, to show otherwise. Even if we knew that race as a scientific concept was a lie, the eyes didn't lie either, Hall observed, and as long as people could see and point out differences in skin color, not to mention hair texture and other physical features, it would be hard to keep them from jumping to conclusions about the sources of those differences and what they thought those differences signified—from group variations in IQ that were supposedly rooted in genetics, to "natural" fitness for the production of culture and the attainment of civilization, an idea as old as the Enlightenment.

What we might think of as "Hall's Dilemma"—the challenge of keeping people from investing meaning into "race" as a category of biological difference, based on superficial differences visible to the eye—is as old as some of the earliest European encounters with "the other" in Africa and the New World in the modern period (beginning five hundred years ago), when differences of culture and phenotype soon fused with economic desire and exploitation to produce "the African" as a new and mostly negative signifier. And for centuries, this toxic compound has played into our very human instinct for defining ourselves through some of our most obvious, often "measurable" differences, such as skin color, cranial size, width of nose, and other body parts, all haphazardly gathered under the category of "race," which itself at various times could either be an amalgam of ethnicity, religion, and nationality, or be separate from each of these.

Through what Hall described as a loose but lethal "chain of equivalences" (a concept he borrowed from the Argentinean political philosopher Ernesto Laclau) drawn between what the eyes could see and what the mind could perceive, hierarchical scaffolding of one kind or another has been erected, with those in power seizing the authority to produce knowledge about what those differences, arbitrarily elevated over others in importance, signified, and then to act on those differences, or that chain of differences, with devastating real-world consequences.

What also intrigued Hall was how oppressed groups themselves, in acts of seeming self-liberation, inverted these categories without discarding them, instead championing racial or ethnic pride as if they believed that after surviving the lethal effects of essentialization, the most efficacious way to defeat, say, anti-black or anti-brown racism or colonialism was to flip the script, embrace physical differences, and essentialize themselves. And so the boundaries of nations-within-nations were drawn, with those at the center and those on the periphery locked in a struggle over power rather than a struggle over the *discursive terms* expressive or reflective of that power. In other words, in a messy world of mixing and migrations, he observes, the boundaries of race, ethnicity, and nationality somehow maintained their distinctiveness—a development that not only offended Hall's cosmopolitan sensibilities but troubled him as he searched for a better, more just, more reliable signifier of cultural difference.

Giving Hall's quest its urgency was the fact that the world in the mid-1990s was rapidly shrinking, with one century giving way to another at a time of increasing technological change, economic interdependence, and mass migration, accompanied by a rise in fundamentalism along racial, ethnic, national, and religious lines. Hall saw pockets of hope in the creative yearnings of marginalized groups laying claim to new "identifications" and "positionalities," and fashioning out of shared historical experience "signi-fiers of a new kind of ethnicized modernity, close to the cutting edge of a new iconography and a new se-miotics that [was] redefining 'the modern' itself" (see Lecture 2)—a theme Hall had explored in his seminal essay "New Ethnicities," first delivered as a conference paper at the Institute of Contemporary Arts in London in 1988.

At the same time, however, he saw that there was cause for grave concern that the world could pull apart along the old, worn-out seams just as it had begun to come together, with rigid categories of ra-cial, ethnic, and national differences only hardening in the face of the prospect—or threat—of meaningful change. Hall "advocated for a different, postcolonial understanding of multiculturalism," the historian James Vernon writes. "It was one that both acknowl-edged and celebrated the hybrid and mongrelized na-ture of cultures that slavery and colonialism had both produced and displaced. Colonial history ensured that it was no longer possible to conceive of specific communities or traditions whose boundaries and identities were settled and fixed."

Realist though Stuart Hall was when it came to the potency and indisputable resiliency of racial, ethnic, and national schemes, as I noted, he did not come to Harvard in April 1994 to replay broken records. Instead, he came, as he said in his first lecture, "to complicate and unsettle" society's persistently held notions of race, ethnicity, and nation—what he referred to in the title of the lecture series as a "fateful triangle"—and to open up new possibilities for defining our twenty-first-century selves. Not only did he teach that those old categories of difference failed to capture the blurriness of human existence, the myriad intersections of identities, pasts, and backgrounds; he also made plain that, in pretending to represent anything close to pure boundaries between groups, those old categories carried with them histories of oppression, perpetuating dangerous group-think while reinforcing hierarchical notions of cultural difference. The slate needed to be wiped clean, and Stuart was holding the eraser.

The setting for his intervention was the trio of W. E. B. Du Bois Lectures that he delivered in Room 105 of Emerson Hall at Harvard University. I know, because I was there. I was then in my third year as director of Harvard's W. E. B. Du Bois Institute for African and African American Research, which each year sponsors the Du Bois Lectures as part of our mission to advance research about the histories and cultures of Africa and the African Diaspora. I was delighted that Stuart had accepted my invitation to speak, and, like the rest of the audience, which included Kwame Anthony Appiah, I was riveted by his imagination and courage in living out the credo he'd imbibed from his intellectual soulmate, Antonio Gramsci, whom he quoted in his second lecture: "pessimism of the intellect and optimism of the will." Genial as he was, Hall was the classic disrupter, eschewing inherited truths in favor of a more open, ceaselessly revisable mode of being in the world—a world which in that era, like today, was shifting beneath our feet.

The mid-1990s was, to borrow a Hallsian phrase, a "conjunctural" moment, when the forces of globalization were simultaneously uprooting and emboldening concepts of racial, ethnic, and nationalist difference across Europe and the United States. Dissatisfied with fighting the same battles on the same terrain, he asked us, in his third lecture, to consider his proposal that the metaphor with the greatest potential to unleash the energies of possibility surrounding populations quickly moving from the peripheries of society to its center was one with a historical arc with which we were already familiar: "diaspora." In our brave new world, "homelessness" was a more apt description of the postmodern condition than was that of laying claim to a home that never really existed in any pure, original state. "Hall's skepticism about essentialism raises the possibility of a conversation that might end in a radical homelessness," Grant Farred writes in his introduction to a 2016 special issue of the *South Atlantic Quarterly* dedicated to Hall. As an immigrant writing about immigrants the world over, Hall's quest was to feel at home without becoming "like" the majority culture. "Articulated through this rejection," Farred explains, "'We are not going to become like you' is the tension that has shaped Hall as a thinker."

For Hall, "diaspora" spoke to the sense of ceaseless movement he saw in the world around him, and it was intertwined with modernity. It also signified belonging to a culture, a tradition, a heritage—a historical arc that bound us together without closing the door to further transformations or other kinships. It was less about origins than trajectories. Hall wasn't interested in simply copying and pasting the metaphor of diaspora onto late-twentieth-century humanity. He wanted to shake it free from its history, both the good and the bad, before offering it up as a new term for new constructions of subjectivity brought on by the new era of globalization. "When I ask someone where they're from, nowadays I expect a very long answer," Hall says in the 2013 documentary film *The Stuart Hall Project*. In his Du Bois Lectures, he gave his response to that phenomenon and thought creatively about how to address it in ways that would empower those who had long been marginalized in battles over religion, science, and multiculturalism. And he did so while standing within the heart of African and African American studies at one of the world's most pluralistic universities.

By title, Hall was professor of sociology and head of the Sociology Department at the Open University in England (which he joined in 1979), having emigrated from his native Jamaica to England in the fall of 1951 to take up studies as a Rhodes Scholar at Merton College, University of Oxford, where he "read" English Literature. Those who studied Stuart Hall as a theorist, those who revered him as a hero, and those who loved him as a teacher and friend knew him as a founding father (along with Richard Hoggart and Raymond Williams) of the field of cultural studies, which he launched as the founding editor of the *New Left Review* in 1960 and, beginning in 1964, as a member of the Centre for Contemporary Cultural Studies at the University of Birmingham, of which he became acting director in 1968 and then director in 1972. He also became known as a steadfast, implacable critic of "Thatcherism."

Margaret Thatcher was leader of the Conservative Party of the United Kingdom from 1975 to 1990 and prime minister from 1979 to 1990, and Stuart Hall was one of her staunchest and most searching critics. Hall's analysis of Mrs. Thatcher's particular brand of conservative politics, known as Thatcherism, then of New Labour and of neoliberalism, began during his time with the *New Left Review*, included work that he and his collaborators did for the book *Policing the Crisis* (1978), and extended through *The Hard Road to Renewal: Thatcherism and the Crisis of the Left,* published a decade later (1988). Hall's political writings and his writings about race and culture are often thought of as parallel discourses, when in fact they were inextricably intertwined, part of the same, larger effort to understand the world in which we were living.

During this time, Hall remained at the forefront of the field of cultural studies, which received a welcome reception among African Americanists, starting in the late 1980s and early 1990s, through collaborations with Autograph ABP (formerly known as the Association of Black Photographers, founded in 1988), and with the Institute of International Visual Arts (Iniva, founded in 1994), and key artists and filmmakers in the British Black Arts Movement, such as Isaac Julien and John Akomfrah, Joy Gregory and Rotomi Fani-Kayode, and curators David A. Bailey, Mark Sealy, and later Renée Mussai. Hall chaired both Autograph ABP and Iniva, which moved into their shared home, designed by Sir David Adjaye, at Rivington Place in 2007. But at the center of the Black Arts Movement stood Stuart Hall, as theorist, mentor, friend, and tutelary spirit, inspiring not only artists and filmmakers but other younger theorists as well, such as Hazel V. Carby, Paul Gilroy, and Kobena Mercer. Moreover, it was he and his works that linked the fields of African American critical studies and black British cultural studies. Just as Hall's work helped to expand the focus of cultural studies to take into account race and gender, so, too, did his work help expand the focus of African American studies to take into account class and cosmopolitan or international definitions of race and ethnicity.

Stuart Hall's written words were ardent, discerning, recondite, and provocative, his spoken voice lyrical, euphonious, passionate, at times rhapsodic, and he changed the way an entire generation of critics and commentators debated issues of race and cultural difference. To keep up with him, you had to be curious and nimble when you entered the room he occupied. He wanted us to question everything, from his subject position(s) to ours.

I first heard of Stuart Hall from Raymond Williams in the course of our "supervision" (tutorial) in Tragedy during the 1973-1974 academic year at Williams's offices at Jesus College, University of Cambridge, where I was reading English Literature, or attempting to, having majored in history as an undergraduate at Yale. It would be another decade, perhaps, before I realized that Stuart Hall was black. If Hall's Jamaican origin struck Professor Williams as important, it was just as important for him, in order to remain true to his Marxist politics and aesthetics, not to mention it—perhaps especially to a young African American. I was simply astonished to learn later that Hall was black, and I find Williams's decision somewhat astonishing, even today, some forty-odd years later. Believe me, I could have used a black signifier when I was struggling to find my way through the jungle of literary theory at the University of Cambridge in the mid-1970s—someone who could have played a similar role as Wole Soyinka and Kwame Anthony Appiah, who guided my way into African studies at the very same time. I shared this story with Stuart the first time we met, in the late eighties, to explain why I hadn't made a pilgrimage from Cambridge up to Birmingham at that time. Somehow, he didn't seem surprised. I think there was a sense in Williams, whom I enormously respected, that if we don't talk about it, "it" doesn't exist.

With Stuart, by contrast, teaching meant keeping as much as possible—as much of our subject positions as we were aware of—out in the open. Nothing was beyond challenge or debate. Angela McRobbie writes in a recent article on Hall's teaching that he was committed to the idea of an "open pedagogy" that looked to engage people outside the elite. "Despite all his important theoretical efforts," Lawrence Grossberg reminds us in an obituary of his one-time mentor, "Stuart was not a philosopher, and certainly not the founder of a philosophical paradigm. He loved theory, but his work was never about theory; it was always about trying to understand and change the realities and possibilities of how people might live together in the world."

Briefly stated, Hall said that his aim in his Du Bois Lectures, delivered at the end of the twentieth century, was to update Du Bois's bold warning from the beginning of that century: "to see the question of ethnicity—alongside and in an uneasy and unresolved relationship to race, on the one hand, and to nation, on the other—as posing a key problem that radically unsettles all three terms. Posing the question in this way presents us with what I see as *the* problem of the twenty-first century—the problem of living with difference—in a manner that is not only analogous to the problem of the 'color line' that W. E. B Du Bois pointed to more than a hundred years ago but also a historically specific transformation of it." No longer historically rooted in the Jim Crow color line of segregation, the problem was about difference writ large; before he could move toward a solution, he wanted to show both the fallacy of relying on the old categories, laced as they were with power, and the risk of courting fundamentalism in defending them, a warning that seems remarkably prophetic today.

In his analysis of the problem, Hall conducted a master class in the operation of each category of difference, showing how superficial differences observed by the eye translated into inferential judgments of the mind that were difficult for even the most talented scholar to dislodge with facts. That didn't keep him from trying. As the cultural theorist Tony Bennett explains in a recent article, in Hall's mind, "the elements comprising any hegemonic formation could always be broken apart, and be given new meanings and political directions, through the conduct of politics as—for Stuart—mainly a set of ideological-discursive struggles." In the case of race and ethnicity and nationhood, Hall was skeptical that any of these discourses could be reappropriated toward sustainable ends. If differences of one kind or another were unavoidable, the choice of metaphors about those differences—and the social and political implications and effects of those metaphors—was not; and at stake was not only semantics, but the spaces those words opened up for new subjectivities and values.

For the anthropologist David Scott, Hall's work, including his landmark essay "New Ethnicities," was defined by "the elements of an ethics of the self and other attuned precisely to the *edges*, the *margins*, where 'identity' ceases to hold with certainty and where ambiguity, otherness, finitude, the outside, begin to decenter and undermine its fables of stable self-presence. Stuart proposes that we take seriously that there is something altogether reductive and *therefore* morally impoverished about the picture of human selves and human interaction that emerges from the one-sided Enlightenment admiration for a sovereign, autonomous self legislating the single good for us all. We stand a chance of flourishing better, he suggests, the more open we can *make* ourselves to our own vulnerability—our own fragile, exposed, receptivity—to difference."

Larry Grossberg, like so many of us in university life, "had never met an academic like this before—humble, generous, passionate, someone who treated everyone with equal respect and listened to what they had to say, someone who believed ideas mattered, *because* of our responsibility as intellectuals to people and the world." Grossberg adds: "Stuart did not teach us what the questions were and certainly [did] not provide the answers. He taught us how to think relationally and contextually, and therefore how to ask questions. He taught us how to think and even live with complexity and difference." Hall didn't offer solutions; he showed us an approach for living in a world of interlacing lives.

"I'm very pleased indeed to be here," Hall declared in the *Harvard Crimson* on the occasion of his Du Bois Lectures in 1994. "The Du Bois Institute in the heart of Harvard is an extremely important political intervention, and I'm delighted to be invited to speak here." But it was I who was even more pleased, I would think. Hosting Stuart Hall at the Du Bois Institute was one of the great intellectual moments of my academic life, and I couldn't be more delighted that Harvard University Press is publishing his lectures. This book will serve both to preserve the memory of that very special moment when, one might say, the field of cultural studies met African and African American studies, and to allow a new generation of scholars to engage with this great thinker's prescient ideas about identity in a globalizing world. I am only sorry that Stuart and his wife Catherine and the faculty of the Department of African and African American Studies can't celebrate the publication of this book together, since Stuart died in 2014, at the age of eighty-two, too soon to see these lectures appear in print.

"Written across Stuart's work, from beginning to end," Homi Bhabha notes in an article on Hall's legacy, "is the belief that culture and politics are practices 'without guarantees.'" That belief was certainly also extended to notions of race, ethnicity, and nationality, however much they persevered in human thought and action. As right as Bhabha is about this lack of guarantees, I can offer readers of this volume one firm guarantee: in the pages that follow, you will be as "complicated and unsettled" by Hall's beautiful mind as we were when we sat riveted in Emerson Hall in Harvard Yard, listening to his every word all those years ago—unsettled, engaged, transformed.

INTRODUCTION

Kobena Mercer

IN *THE FATEFUL TRIANGLE* Stuart Hall disentangles the interlocking categories of race, ethnicity, and nation. All three classify the immense diversity of human life. But with their deadly and divisive consequences, one might ask if our lives would not be better without them. However, what kind of human has an unraced, unethnic, or unnational identity? In the face of such questions, Hall invites us to see matters in a fresh light. What confronts us, he argues, are the three historical forms taken by the discourses of cultural difference as they have interwoven with relations of power throughout the modern age. Hitherto unpublished, his W. E. B. Du Bois Lectures delivered at Harvard University in April 1994 vividly illuminate the political implications of Hall's theoretical position. He reveals that the agency of difference, which operates in all discourse, is both the reason social institutions strive for fixity and the condition by which subjects break out of oppression to make their entrance into history. With quiet rigor, Hall states the case for a discursive conception of cultural identity. The critical steps taken in his careful reasoning give us the tools to loosen the Gordian knot that has shadowed global modernity from the start.

In the renowned Du Bois lecture series, hosted by Harvard's Department of African and African American Studies, scholars engage issues of lifelong concern to W. E. B. Du Bois, who earned his doctorate at the institution in 1895. Du Bois devoted his life to transforming the self-perception of societies shaped by the realities of race, whether in America, Europe, Africa, or Asia, and his intellectual output embodied the critical cosmopolitanism he acquired as a result. Hall's first lecture strikes up a conversation with Du Bois over troubling ambiguities in the concept of race that have vexed eminent thinkers for well over a century. Drawing on his life's journey from colonial Jamaica to postempire Britain, Hall's second and third lectures look into what is new and distinctive about the politics of ethnicity and the predicament of nation-states under the pressures of globalization at the end of the twentieth century, offering a late modern reprise of the world-minded outlook that informed all of his commitments as a diasporic intellectual.

Based on his handwritten lecture notes and amended transcripts, *The Fateful Triangle* adds a vital chapter to Hall's oeuvre. It offers a succinct distillation of the fertile development that his thinking on race, ethnicity, and nation went through as issues of diaspora came to the forefront of his work in the late 1980s and early 1990s. Hall had addressed questions of race from the outset of his career, yet in contrast to the sociological orientation of his early work and his focus on the articulation of race, class, and the state in the 1970s, the first lecture, "Race—The Sliding Signifier," presents us with a concentrated account of why the race concept stubbornly persists, despite every demystification showing its realities to be socio-historical and not biological. Hall's close attention to the driving force of difference in the discursive production of meaning gives us a genealogy that reveals the world-making work performed by a category that, although scientifically void, possesses an extraordinary degree of symbolic resourcefulness in giving order to the fluctuating conditions of social life. By virtue of its binary codification of the world, race makes meaning out of the arbitrary variations of human phenotype. But it is precisely these meanings—not any biogenetic materials—that are contested in political struggle.

Today one finds widespread, if not universal, agreement for the view that race is but a social construction, yet Hall asks us to think carefully about what it means to take up such a stance. Where the concept of "race" stands discredited by science, many argue we should adopt the concept of "ethnicity" instead. However, in Hall's second lecture, "Ethnicity and Difference in Global Times," his discursive method of analysis reveals why such a seemingly straightforward solution is thwarted by the realities of political life. Where group membership defined by shared language, custom, religion, and belief creates symbolic communities out of purely cultural materials, Hall observes two modes in the discursive formation of ethnicity. Closed forms, in which a strong sense of belonging is grounded in a geographic sense of place that excludes what is foreign or alien, often entail potent invocations of "kith and kin" or "blood and soil," which seek to fix the meaning of *ethnos* in essentialist and transcendentalist terms. In this respect, closed discourses of ethnicity stake all-or-nothing claims on the unchangeable realm of nature in exactly the same way as racial discourse does. Showing that clear-cut distinctions between "ethnicity" and "race" get undermined in the push toward group closure, Hall's example of the alternative form, in which open constructions of ethnicity are produced, is highly revealing. In the alliances that Afro-Caribbean and South Asian communities forged in antiracist struggles in postwar Britain, the term "black" became the signifier of an emergent identity that arose not from any basis in genetics, nor from shared customs, but from the discursive slide whereby contested meanings that gathered under the markers of cultural difference served to expand the ground on which political antagonism to the status quo was articulated. Where open-ended forms treat the boundaries of belonging as permeable, new ethnicities do not seek to eternalize identity in myths of purity and origin that rely on exclusionary closure against difference, but instead accept that all collective identifications are subject to fluctuating historical conditions. Developing far-reaching insights from this concrete historical analysis, Hall maps out such world-turning consequences of migration in his third lecture, "Nations and Diasporas."

Nation-states that acquired modern form in the 1700s had narrative as an indispensable medium, Hall suggests, in calling vast numbers of disparate people into a shared identification. To grasp the discursive figure of the "freeborn Englishman," for instance, as a product of this historical moment is to agree that such an identity depended on his difference from colonial and enslaved others who were excluded from any "natural rights." Yet to follow this genealogy into the present is to recognize that such a figure was never an illusion or a textual fiction but an anchoring point for processes of collective identification that have been ripped apart and thrown into crisis as a consequence of today's capitalist globalization. To the extent that identity is dependent on coordinates of space and time in order to create a sense of location—of having a place called home—the hypermobility with which money, goods, information, and people now circulate on our ever more interconnected planet results in the massive dislocation of anchoring points within the symbolic order of culture. Where migrants are the target of choice for new racisms in contemporary Europe and the United States, the dislocation brought about by economic deregulation is encoded in narratives that represent cultural difference as incompatibly other to the nation, thereby leading to xenophobic forms of group closure. However, where culture itself travels as a result of migration, diaspora formations that

arise with the scattering of people from their place
of origin carry the promise of other ways of dealing
with difference. Subjects forced to migrate from
one cultural context to another not only have to
speak several different languages to ensure their
survival but also are obliged to "translate" between
them, and in the process hybrid mixtures are created in which all of the identities brought into the
discursive commons are opened to possibilities of
transculturation.

But diaspora is not a panacea. What Hall finds in
the diaspora formations on which Caribbean history
was built (where his third lecture concludes) is an
understanding of culture itself as a practice of articulation. African, European, American, and Amerindian
elements were combined for centuries in stultifying
hierarchies under the closed order of colonial power.
When postindependence Caribbean nations rede-
fined their identities, what emerged did not arise ex
nihilo; yet an irrevocable rupture with the past was
indeed brought about as the region's constitutive
cultural "presences" became rearticulated into new
configurations. The concept of diaspora underwent a
paradigm shift in the extraordinarily productive
mid-1990s moment when these lectures were conceived. Hall's thinking on cultural politics was

critically enlivened by his engagement with black British artists, filmmakers, and photographers, and by Paul Gilroy's 1993 book, *The Black Atlantic: Modernity and Double Consciousness,* whose radical impact is acknowledged throughout these lectures.[1] Reconceptualizing diaspora not as a tragic loss of organic *roots* but as a polycentric network of cross-cultural *routes* that give black culture its transnational dynamism, the "black Atlantic" model was taken to heart by readers across the globe as the internationalization of cultural studies gained ground in humanities and social science disciplines. However, the extent to which the U.S. reception of Hall's scholarship tended to overlook the key concept of "articulation" in his sociological texts such as "Pluralism, Race, and Class in Caribbean Society" (1978) and "Race, Articulation, and Societies Structured in Dominance" (1980) requires comment, as this earlier body of work laid the basis for the relational mode in which Hall has always conceptualized race, ethnicity, and nation.[2]

Understanding the economic, political, and cultural spheres of a social formation to be relatively autonomous instances that work together, or get articulated, "to provide the conditions of existence of any conjuncture," Hall departed from the reductive determinism of base/superstructure thinking in Marxist traditions.[3] His structuralist method of approach meant that instead of being an organic totality, society is conceived as a combinatory structure whose constitutive instances are open to contingency. Contradictory pressures arise among the instances and contribute to turning points of historical rupture and social transformation, but the outcomes to historical crises cannot be predetermined, as the contingent factor means there will always be a struggle, an antagonism, over how dominant and subordinate elements come to be rearticulated.

Far from being an abstract exercise, *Policing the Crisis* (1978) revealed race as an irreducible element in Britain's crisis of consensus that led to the law-and-order policies of the Thatcher years.[4] The concept of "the ethnic signifier" that Hall introduced in his 1978 text on Caribbean society anticipated his turn toward poststructuralist methods in the 1980s. It is crucial, therefore, to acknowledge the framework of articulatory practice that provides architectonic grounding for the discursive models through which Hall continued to examine lines of power and resistance inscribed by race, ethnicity, and nation.

Migration matters decisively in *The Fateful Triangle*—being the flash point around which ethnic chauvinisms, neonationalisms, and numerous fundamentalisms strive to close down the symbolic boundaries of group belonging—but Hall's optimistic claims for the alternative that diaspora cultures embody are emphatically materialist. In Hall's brand of cultural studies, culture always has a material existence—not as a collection of discrete texts or stand-alone artifacts but as the key instance of the social formation in which emergent forces first make their presence felt as they come up against dominant and residual blocs of established authority. In setting his sights on crisis moments "where cultural processes anticipate social change," Hall directs our attention to surfaces of emergence that give us analytical access to the potential for transformation latent in each historical conjuncture.[5] It is the way in which an era's conflicted irresolution—its crisis—comes to be symbolized, imagined, and represented in the cultural realm that influences how ordinary men and women act upon antagonisms that are alive and up for grabs precisely because the manner of their articulation cannot be determined in advance by any historical telos. In today's global politics of identity and difference, the migrant condition is symptomatically central for

Hall, for it speaks through a "double syntax" in which difference may be driven toward the all-or-nothing dangers of ethnic absolutism—or it may, if we seize the opportunity, enable us to learn something from diasporic survival about how to live with others and otherness.

The happenstance by which *The Fateful Triangle* lectures went unpublished during Hall's lifetime has resulted in a delay of twenty-plus years that only serves to heighten the prescience of his thinking in 1994. In light of events, from 9/11 in New York City to the Syrian refugee crisis that erupted in 2015, no one would dispute his prophetic claim that the growing proliferation of antagonism around cultural difference is *the* defining political question of our times. It is because the driving contradictions that shape our present are all too alive in their irresolution that there is urgency in our need to grasp how culture and politics are intricately articulated in struggles over difference and identity today. If some retreat into culture for fear that the politics of identity is unresolvable, *The Fateful Triangle* upholds the intellectual vocation of cultural studies, which is to lay bare the conditions that define contemporaneity as an impasse to be overcome. Yet this is to say that the time gap between the conception and publication of *The Fateful Triangle* provides a lens through which to see that what makes these lectures unique is the incisive economy with which they sum up what is at stake politically in making a commitment to the argument that our lived experience of collective belonging—as it is coded by race, ethnicity, and nation—is open to change precisely because it is constructed *discursively*.

To the extent that constructionism has become the default setting for today's humanities, is it fair to say the apparent acceptance that every identity is a construct has come at the cost of an ethics of critique? To agree that differences—of gender, sexuality, and disability as much as race or culture—have been constructed in oppressive ways that delimit human freedom is to take a stance in which the whole point of *de*constructing such iniquitous structures is to create alternatives in which it becomes possible to *re*articulate difference equitably. But under global conditions of neoliberalism, the focus of Hall's political analysis throughout the 1990s and 2000s, it is as if images of abundance and inclusion we access through our digital screens act as a spectacle, culturally, which hides from view social divisions and economic disparities that have grown ever deeper in the past quarter century.[6] Over the last two decades of his life, Hall's writings on the visual arts, on globalization, and on neoliberalism consistently addressed ethnicity, race, and nation as they weave in and out of the cultural politics of identity. But what makes *The Fateful Triangle* such a singular gift from Hall's archive is that in his genealogy of global modernity he demonstrates that the tools that best serve the task of taking apart the overdetermined knot that placed race, ethnicity, and nation at the heart of our experience of collective belonging are to be found in discursive models of difference. Touching on just a few of the seams of inquiry opened up by Hall's step-by-step approach to discursive constructionism, I would like to set the context for a small number of the many conceptual resources *The Fateful Triangle* offers us for disentangling twenty-first-century culture and politics.[7]

Few today would say pigmentation tells us anything about intelligence, for example, but the fact that we notice a person's skin color is, as Hall points out, an outcome of the "traces" deposited in everyday ways of seeing and knowing by the history of racial discourse. While this explains why Du Bois did not abandon the race concept, even though he was among the first to doubt its scientific validity, it is also why Hall disagrees with Anthony Appiah's view that Du Bois should have completed the anti-biologistic argument by renouncing the very idea of "race" altogether. Whereas Appiah's primary concern is with the referential dimension of language, and turns on a model in which true meaning depends on a one-to-one correspondence between words and things, from which perspective race is a category error, Hall's emphasis is on the primacy of the signifier. In Ferdinand de Saussure's view that "in language there are only differences without positive terms," arbitrary graphemes and phonemes (signifiers) come to be correlated with cognitive content (signifieds) only on the basis of conventions that speakers implicitly share as they exchange signs.[8] For meaning to be possible, the "differencing" activity whereby phonemes and graphemes undergo a potentially infinite range of paradigmatic and syntagmatic permutations before the unity of the sign is fixed means that the signifier's movement in the signifying chain takes precedence, because it is only after signs are agreed by convention that they acquire referents. The implications of Hall's starting point are far-reaching indeed.

With citations of Bartolomé de Las Casas in 1550 and Edmund Burke in 1777, Hall shows that binary lines of religious debate about racial difference, which led Europeans to think of New World peoples as a separate species, are reinscribed in the dividing line between "civilization" and "barbarism" as defined by natural philosophy and science during the Enlightenment. Instead of a mimetic relationship in which words reflect things given in nature, Hall explains the process in which as every discourse constructs its referent as an object of knowledge, it thereby renders reality available to relations of power. "Discourse is about the production of knowledge in language," he states. "But . . . since all social practices entail meaning, and meanings shape and influence what we do—our conduct—all practices have a discursive aspect."[9]

With the binary encoding by which race establishes orders of meaning over the world's fluctuating contingency, racial discourse brings a vast array of heterogeneous phenomena into a common grid of intelligibility within which signifiers are fixed along "chains of equivalence." With a light touch that belies the gravity of his insight, Hall reads the semiotics of phenotype—the bodily signifiers encapsulated in Frantz Fanon's phenomenology of the colonial gaze— in terms of visual differences that are made meaningful when read *down* the signifying chain as markers of biogenetic essences, coded as all the more un-changeable because they are invisible. Conversely, when read *up* the chain, these visible differences of race connote civilizational accomplishment, folk spirit, and other intangible qualities that carry all the more symbolic weight because they too are inaccessible to the eye. The poststructuralist turn in African American studies led by Henry Louis Gates, Jr., and others is deepened when Hall shows, from his point of view, just what metaphor and metonymy can do.

To the extent that the differencing activity of the signifying chain takes precedence, the poststructuralist critique of the unity of the sign reveals that the permutations of paradigmatic and syntagmatic substitutions and combinations can be a potentially infinite process of semiosis if the point at which the signifying chain is fixed and brought to closure is delayed or deferred. For Hall, the agency by which "difference" activates the polysemic properties of language entails that every institution and organized activity that claims authority must make an ongoing effort to contain the multidirectional possibilities of semiosis. Limiting the free play of the signifier thus depends entirely on where the caption points are placed on the signifying chain in order to establish fixity on signifying material that is, in its own right, inherently polyvalent in character.

Observing the multiple and often contradictory meanings that the concept of "race" acquired in the age of empire, historian Catherine Hall underlines the point that because of "the fundamentally dialogic character of all interactions, and the impossibility of finally determining how meanings were received," such multiaccentuality is of profound importance politically, for it shows that there is always "the possibility of struggle over meanings."[10] It is precisely the possibility of breaking with oppressive regimes of racial meaning that is at stake in the polysemic agency of difference, which makes discourse the medium in which historically subordinated subjects can transform the dominant code and activate resistance, not by going outside it to speak in a completely different language, which would be unintelligible, but by relocating the caption point at which the slide of signification is brought to a close in the articulation of mutually intelligible signs.

Long after Du Bois moved from an uplift standpoint to a leftist one, his 1940 statement in *Dusk of Dawn* that "race" defines a collective identity based on shared heritage makes no referential sense in biogenetic terms. If the concept "binds together not simply the children of Africa, but extends through yellow Asia and into the South Seas," we must be in the presence of a sliding signifier that has been disarticulated or unfixed from its previous signified, and now rearticulated to an alternative meaning by virtue of a game-changing move that has relocated the caption point in the signifying chain.[11] To articulate African, African American, Asian, and Pacific identities, as Du Bois did, is to construct a chain of equivalence that subverts the binary code so as to posit instead a countervailing set of anticolonial alliances. When Hall turns his attention to the meaning of "black" as a subject position taken up by Afro-Caribbeans and Asians against residual blocs of discrimination in U.K. society, he reveals that this transformational act of resignification—which is irreducibly discursive—is the generative source from which political rupture and social change is born.

Hall's close attention to the materiality of discourse in *The Fateful Triangle* thus clarifies two prevalent misconceptions about the discursive constructionist model. Contrary to the view that we have a choice between fixed and unfixed discourses, the moment of closure *must* take place, for without it no correlation between signifier and signified can be established. Taking great pains to be clear, Hall asks, "Is it possible for there to be action or identity in the world without arbitrary closure—what one might call the necessity to meaning of the end of the sentence?" He thus made the all-important contrast between a provisional mode of temporary closure that is receptive to revision, thereby staying open-ended, and an approach that aims for absolute finality in its quest to fix the polysemic slide of the signifying chain. Where "all the social movements which have tried to transform society, and have required the constitution of new subjectivities, have had to accept . . . the arbitrary closure, which is not the end but which makes both politics and identity possible," Hall's distinction falls between radical democratic modes of articulation, which expand chains of equivalence so they are capable of including multiple identities around a political demand, and authoritarian modes of closure, in which the unfulfillable quest for finality inexorably leads to violence against that which is expelled from discourse into its "outside" as the unrepresentable and unthinkable other.[12]

If we keep this contrast in view as he examines the "return of ethnicity" in the late twentieth century and the collapse of sovereign boundaries on the part of the modern nation-state, we see that Hall's insights arise from a stance in which, contrary to the misconception that there is nothing outside the text, "all I mean is that no practice is ultimately understandable outside of the context of its meaning. All human practices are embedded in meaning, which is not to say that there is nothing but meaning."[13] As the constitutive ground on which the world becomes actionable on account of the condition of shared intelligibility it establishes among social actors, the discursive medium in which relations of power are articulated among dominant and subordinate identities is also the signifying field on which identities are opened to possibilities of repositioning by virtue of the slide at play in every discourse.

In the second lecture, Hall observes that, despite different historical conditions, movements for racial justice in the United States and the United Kingdom were deeply skeptical about the very concept of "ethnicity." America's self-perception as a multiethnic society shaped by a nation of immigrants dates to the 1920s, yet the liberal discourse of cultural pluralism excluded citizens of African descent, for it drew a line of closure limited to "white ethnics" and religious tolerance. Multiculturalism was rejected by antiracist movements in 1970s Britain, which decried it for deflecting attention from structural inequalities faced by migrants from former colonies. But what Hall finds most striking about today's proliferation of hyphenated identities—whether French Algerian, Turkish German, or black British in Europe, for instance, or Asian American, Latino/a American, or Afro-Canadian in North America, to name but a few, all being symptoms of ethnicity's return under postcolonial and post-civil-rights conditions—is that their celebratory affirmation of difference contravenes the liberal narrative that held that particularistic attachments would eventually be given up in favor of a civic rationality based on universalist principles.

Many agree that the 1960s mark the turning point when the demand for equality gave way to the assertion of difference, but what specifically does discursive constructionism bring to understanding the conditions that precipitated this rupture? While those on the left end of the spectrum lament the demise of collectivist solidarity and interpret difference as colluding with consumerist atomization, with those on the right apportioning responsibility for the collapse of the center ground to the so-called minorities themselves, Hall gives us two sight lines from which to grasp matters anew. The dislocation brought about by globalization takes up the latter part of his analysis, but he starts with Afro-Asian "black" as a new ethnicity whose emergence reveals something hitherto unnoticed in the genealogy of mainstream liberalism.

Facing discrimination in all walks of life, migrants who journeyed into postwar Britain under the auspices of the 1948 Nationality Act, which granted colonial subjects right of entry to the United Kingdom, found themselves in for a shock. A common history of colonial experience meant that most migrants were highly knowledgeable about Britishness, and expected to be treated accordingly, yet with the grim reality of riots in 1958 and the rise of Enoch Powell a decade later, the postempire racism they met indicated the fading of the liberal dream of assimilation. Reading this postassimilationist moment as signaling "the break with the discourse of Enlightenment universalism and liberal humanism on which, up to that point, struggles of resistance had been predicated," Hall takes us through a historiographic move analogous to a cinematic jump cut. The shock that Afro-Asian settlers experienced was a long-distance echo of the answer Toussaint L'Ouverture received from the National Assembly in 1791 when Haiti petitioned for the abolition of slavery on the basis of the universal rights of man, only to have any claim to equality denied on grounds of cultural difference. What Hall brings to light beneath the universalist ideal of equality is an assimilationist particularism built on the basis of the "us" and "them" binary coding of race. Access to the human, in other words, had always been conditional on being the "civilized" and not the "barbarian."

In 2000 Hall surveyed the "multicultural question" in a text that parsed "the subaltern proliferation of difference" comprehensively, although in *The Fateful Triangle* we get to the gist.[14] Making rights of citizenship conditional upon cultural homogeneity, liberal universalism turned on an assimilationist equation in which becoming modern politically meant becoming Western culturally. In the two centuries, circa 1789 to 1989, during which its narratives were held intact by Eurocentric ideologies, the unspoken norm was that humanity was indelibly marked by the "us"/"them" boundary put into place by the binary codes of racial discourse. This unspeakable nucleus of disavowal was what burst apart with decolonization and the social movements of the 1960s.

To get a sense of how deeply this equation was embedded, consider the tough task that Stuart Hall faced in honoring his friend Raymond Williams, a founding figure in British cultural studies. Williams's organicist view of community belonging, as distinct from mere citizenship, meant that bonds of togetherness depended on generational and geographic continuities that de facto excluded migrants, whose lives are on the move. Calling out this assumption, Hall insisted, "It should not be necessary to look, walk, feel, think, or speak exactly like a . . . 'freeborn Englishman' *culturally* to be accorded either the informal courtesy and respect of civilized social intercourse or the rights of entitlement and citizenship."[15] Indeed, with Hall's contrast between closed and open codings of cultural difference, we can see that assimilationist and absolutist versions of ethnicity each begin to slide toward a strong construction of *ethnos* that must close off its borders if its precarious composition of collective identity is to stay whole.

But can cultures of hybridity be entirely responsible for articulating more livable forms of imagined community? The antihybridity backlash of the mid-1990s, which saw the hopes invested in hyphenated identities eclipsed by the rise of Islamic fundamentalism, led social scientists to deem cultural studies irrelevant to the problems of British Muslims or the plight of Somali refugees.[16] But purely empirical approaches tend to lose sight of the principle Hall acts on at all times, namely, that by identifying the double-edged valence of the contradictory forces at work in the overall conjuncture, we understand culture not as an answer to political predicaments but as the access point to a bigger picture of crisis conditions whose ir-resolution means the present is still open to the un-predictable factor of contingency. In 1998, which marked the fiftieth anniversary of the arrival of the ship *Empire Windrush*, bringing one of the first large groups of Jamaican migrants to Britain, the official inquiry into the death of the black teenager Stephen Lawrence attributed his death to institutional racism in London's Metropolitan Police. Hall's attunement to such fault lines, which are "doubly inscribed by the simultaneous vibrancy of hybridisation and the per-vasiveness of racism," is amplified to a global scale in *The Fateful Triangle* lectures, which also locate the con-tradictions of globalization in the *longue durée* of a world-historical perspective.[17]

The observable costs of dislocation in the postin-dustrial world were set in motion—from Detroit to Rochdale—by neoliberal economics, but why, Hall asks in his third lecture, has cultural difference featured so prominently in the specifically political response that takes the form of religious fundamen-talisms, whether Islamic or Christian, ethnonation-alisms in postcommunist Eastern Europe, or ugly

"Little Englandism"? For all their vastly different content, these trends are symptoms of the breakup of the nation-state in its classical form.

Agreeing with historians of nationalism such as Ernest Gellner and Benedict Anderson that nations are precarious constructions by virtue of their inventedness, Hall integrates race and ethnicity where Marxist historiography left them out because his discursive framework highlights the ambivalent polysemy by which the building blocks of national belonging can go either way politically, depending on how they are articulated. Gellner's view, that nations provided a "roof" under which political rights were granted on condition of cultural sameness, is something Hall regards as underplaying the brute coercion with which, in the case of the United Kingdom, Scots, Welsh, and Irish ethnicities were subjugated to Englishness as the culturally dominant identity that sought to bind the nation. Moreover, by highlighting the specifically *cultural* materials upon which all collective identifications are built, "Nations and Diasporas" makes the all-important point that identity does not come first, as a prime mover in political action that is then reflected in representation, but is itself dependent on coordinates of space and time that create a sense of having a secure place in the world. With such coordinates now torn apart as a consequence of dislocations wrought by "the global postmodern," the fissile nature of what was previously stitched together, or "sutured," into constructions of mass identity becomes available to authoritarian chains of equivalence that are all the more dangerous because they rely on an other who serves as the enemy around which broken ties of belonging are to be unified.

Unlike the liberal humanist view of the individual as the source and origin of meaningful action, the decentered subject examined in poststructuralist terms, who is dependent on language, discourse, and representation to provide the positions from which action and practice are guided by meaning, is also dependent at all times on that which is "not self," for what is other to me is the precondition of the "I" who becomes a self only by making its way into language. Running underneath Hall's symptomatic reading of why cultural difference is so highly charged in the crisis conditions of our present is his unflinching insight that the decentered subject is not just fissile— liable to break apart under pressures that consciousness misrecognizes—but that when it is desutured from its moorings in space and time, which provide identities with the necessary fiction of self-sufficient coherence, what we find behind the ego's mask is the human capacity for violence. Like its twin, desire, such aggression can never be fully satisfied, for it stems from the lack, the realm of the "not me," which is the ground on which the human is built.

In his 2007 conversation "Living with Difference," Hall was emphatic that the question of how "to make some kind of common life" calls on us to engage in discursive practices that "depend on a trade-off, a conversation, a process of translation." "If I give up my burka will you give up your union jack?" he asked. "What is the difference that I'm willing to die for? . . . Or am I willing to have a trade-off?" He pointed out that as global forces throw "cultures contradictorily together . . . even as multiculturalism is . . . trying to manage the problems which globalization has created," the countervailing logic of translation in diaspora cultures of hybridity offers an interpretive key with which to practice the politics of difference as an ongoing negotiation of reciprocal give-and-take.

Art is the one sphere in culture where the unspeakable fears and fantasies invested in the violence unleashed upon otherness and difference can be brought into discourse and rendered speakable, for "in art things get said in ways in which they can't get said in any other domain." To the extent that "art arises from experience, is at the same time different from experience, and reflects critically back on it," it is less a mirror of reality than a detour through the fissile stuff of which the human subject is made, since art "addresses your subjective investments in ways over which you have less control, in ways that are less ... under the rational inspection of your purposes and intentions."[18] When Bill Schwarz says, "There is today so much obeisance to the idea of multiculturalism that those domains in our lives which remain trenchantly untransformed, still subject to a racial or colonial logic ... lack the requisite vocabularies with which make them speakable," we come to see why Hall's late-period commitment to the visual arts follows directly from his constructionist trajectory.[19] The polysemic agency of difference that authoritative discourse strives to close down and contain in absolute fixity is precisely what art loosens up so as to render imaginable, and thus tangible, alternative rearticulations in the signifying field, as Hall elucidates in his 2009 video interview when he segues from "difference and multiculturalism" to "race, diaspora, and art."[20]

Instead of striving for all-or-nothing finality in the heterogeneity of human life, Hall invites us to embrace the source of the optimism he found in translation. To translate is to *move across,* which is what the migrant does as a double-facing figure, looking both ways. Yes, there is always something left over in translation. But, far from being a deficit or a minus, what eludes language—what resists capture by prevailing codes and conventions—enlivens the extra or the surplus, thus ensuring that the dialogue is kept open, kept in motion.

1

RACE—THE SLIDING SIGNIFIER

IN THESE THREE lectures I will try to bring to bear on questions of race, ethnicity, nations, and diaspora some thinking that tries not to replicate what distinguished African American scholars could do but offers a view from another part of the black Atlantic world, setting the issues in a wider, global context. I want to reflect on the nature of cultural difference as it is constructed in a variety of discourses. I ought to say from the outset that I'll use the word *discourse* perhaps ad nauseam, yet by it I mean not a set of textual pyrotechnics but rather an overall view of human conduct as always meaningful. As we set out to ask what it means to rethink cultural difference in discursive terms, discourse should be understood as that which gives human practice and institutions meaning, that which enables us to make sense of the world, and hence that which makes human practices meaningful practices that belong to history precisely because they signify in the way they mark out human

differences. I want to submit the three terms of cultural difference at stake in the title of my lectures—
race, ethnicity, nation—to a discursive-genealogical
analysis in light of certain political and theoretical
concerns, and to also use each term to complicate and
unsettle the others a little.

In this first lecture, I want to return, at what you
might think is a late stage in the game, to the question of what we might mean by saying that race is a
cultural and historical, not biological, fact—that race
is a discursive construct, a sliding signifier. Though
such statements have almost acquired the status of a
canonical orthodoxy in some advanced circles, critics
and theorists do not always mean the same thing or
draw the same conceptual and political inferences
from it. The idea that race is discursively constructed
has not, in my experience, done very effectively
the work of unhinging and dislodging commonsense assumptions—ways of talking about, making
sense of, or calculating for the great, untidy, "dirty"
world of everyday life outside the academy. Nor have
its dislocating effects on political mobilization or on
the assessment of the strategies of antiracist politics
been adequately charted.

I refer to "race" here as one of those major or master
concepts (the masculine form is deliberate) that or-

ganize the great classificatory systems of difference that operate in human societies. Race, in this sense, is the centerpiece of a hierarchical system that produces differences. These are differences, moreover, of which W. E. B. Du Bois once said, in 1897, that "subtle, delicate and elusive though they may be . . . [they] have silently but definitively separated men into groups."[1] To say it is one of the great classificatory systems of meaning is to put it neutrally. However, I do this not because I wish in any way to downplay the horrendous human and historical consequences that have followed from the application of this racialized classifying system to social life and to individual men and women, but because I want to insist that, hateful as racism may be as a historical fact, it is nevertheless also a *system of meaning,* a way of organizing and meaningfully classifying the world. Thus any attempt to contest racism or to diminish its human and social effects depends on understanding how exactly this system of meaning works, and why the classificatory order it represents has so powerful a hold on the human imagination.

To put it crudely, the discursive conception of race—as the central term organizing the great classificatory systems of difference in modern human history—recognizes that all attempts to ground the concept scientifically, all efforts to fix the idea of race foundationally on biological, physiological, or genetic grounds, have been shown to be untenable. We must therefore contemplate "substituting a socio-historical and cultural definition of 'race' for the biological one," as the philosopher Anthony Appiah put it in his renowned and elegantly argued essay, "The Uncompleted Argument: Du Bois and the Illusion of Race," in the landmark issue of *Critical Inquiry,* "'Race,' Writing, and Difference," edited by Henry Louis Gates, Jr.[2] In my remarks that follow I want to explore this proposition further. As we know, human genetic variability *between* populations that are normally assigned to a racial category is not significantly greater than variability *within* such populations. What Du Bois, in his essay "The Conservation of Races," called "the grosser physical differences of color, hair and bone," although "clearly defined to the eye of the Historian and Sociologist"[3]—a phrase to which I will return—are, on the one hand, poorly correlated with genetic differences scientifically defined, and are, on the other, impossible to correlate significantly with cultural, social, intellectual, or cognitive characteristics, which means that such "grosser physical differences" are subject to extraordinary variation within any one family, let alone any of the so-called family of races.

I want to make three observations, in passing, about this general position. First, it represents the now common and conventional wisdom among the great majority of scientists in the field. Second, this fact about human genetic variability has never prevented intense scholarly activity among a minority of scientists devoted to the attempt to prove that there is a correlation between racially categorized genetic characteristics and cultural performance—and such activity is once again in full flood today, powered by the rise of the new genome research. Third, I observe that, although the racializing implications of the continuing scientific effort to prove a correlation between, say, race and intelligence are vociferously opposed and condemned by many, including the liberal professions and most black people, nevertheless a great deal of what is routinely said by such groups among and about themselves is predicated precisely on some such assumption. Behind the idea that some social, political, moral, or aesthetic characteristic or phenomenon associated with black people can guarantee the rightness of a political strategy, the correctness of an attitude, or the value of a cultural production, we find the assumption that the truth of such a strategy or attitude or artwork is fixed by the racial characteristics of the participants involved. I deduce from this the awkward insight that diametrically opposed political positions can indeed be derived from the same philosophical foundations, and that although genetic explanations of social behavior are often denounced as racist, nevertheless we find that genetic, biological, and physiological definitions of race are alive and well in the commonsense discourse of us all. This is the paradox my lecture addresses.

The problem with moving to a sociohistorical or cultural conception of racial classification and identification from a genetic or biological one is, as Appiah clearly understood, what to do about the biological trace that remains in racialized discourse today. If I can briefly remind you of his complex and sophisticated argument, Appiah shows that Du Bois, who called his life story the "autobiography of a race concept,"[4] took up positions in which he "came gradually, though never completely, to assimilate the unbiological nature of races."[5] In his 1897 text "The Conservation of Races," Du Bois recognized that although the "subtle, delicate and elusive" differences that have separated humans into groups have sometimes "followed the natural cleavage of common blood, descent and physical peculiarities," they have "at other times swept across and ignored these." The division into races, which we persist in making, is, Du Bois says, something that "perhaps transcend[s] scientific definition."[6] Du Bois thus established early on that "'race' is not a scientific—that is, biological—concept," but Appiah argues that this recognition by Du Bois only partially supersedes the biological, since "if he has fully transcended the scientific notion, what is the role of this talk about 'blood'?" What else, Appiah asks, does "common blood" mean for Du Bois except something "dressed up with fancy craniometry, a dose of melanin, and some measure for hair curl, [which] is what the scientific notion amounts to"?[7] Not only do I agree with this reading of Du Bois's struggle with the race concept, but I also note how symptomatic it is of racial discourse per se that the physical or biological trace, having been shown out of the front door, tends to sidle around the edge of the veranda and climb back in through the pantry window!

As we follow Appiah's analysis and turn to Du Bois's *Crisis* article of 1911, "Races," we find Du Bois moving decisively toward speaking "of civilizations where we now speak of races" when he adds that even "the physical characteristics, excluding the skin color . . . are to no small extent the direct result of the physical and social environment," as well as being "too indefinite and elusive to serve as a basis for any rigid classification or division of human groups."[8] On the basis of this environmental or civilizational emphasis in his thinking, we find that by the time we get to *Dusk of Dawn* in 1940 Du Bois abandons the "scientific" definition in favor of what seems to be a very different argument altogether. Africans and people of African descent may share a common racial ancestry, Du Bois argues, and he says of himself and of his "ancestors going back a thousand years or more" that the "mark of their heritage is upon me in color and hair." He then states, "These are obvious things, but of *little meaning in themselves;* only important as they stand for real and more subtle differences from other men." This represents a critical shift of fundamental importance, for what does matter for Du Bois now, what constitutes the bond between African Americans like him and Africa, is the fact that "these ancestors of mine and their other descendants have had a common history; have suffered a common disaster and have one long memory." "The real essence of this kinship," he concludes, "is its social heritage of slavery."[9] Physical characteristics of "color, hair and bone," as he put it in 1897, which form "the physical bond," are important for Du Bois in 1940 only insofar as they are a "mark" of heritage, with "color relatively unimportant save as a badge." Or, to translate Du Bois into my terms, the "mark" and the "badge" are all-important because they signify, because they carry a certain meaning, because they are, in other words, *signifiers of difference.*

Appiah is certainly right to point out two important aspects of this shift in Du Bois's thinking. First, as Du Bois himself observes, the later definition— "race" as badge—tends to make the concept slip and slide. For, having been loosened from its physiological moorings, Du Bois says of the "social heritage of slavery" that it "binds together not simply the children of Africa, but extends through yellow Asia and into the South Seas. It is this unity that draws me to Africa."[10] But, one is tempted to ask, which unity? Is it biological kinship or political affiliation that Du Bois is addressing? Second, as Appiah pithily remarks, if obvious physical qualities such as the "grosser physical differences of color, hair and bone" are now of "little meaning," then Du Bois's very mention of them in *Dusk of Dawn* marks, on the surface of his argument, the extent to which he still cannot quite escape the appeal of the earlier concept of race.[11]

To put the matter more generally, for it concerns something that affects the entire discourse of race to this day, the fact is that the biological remains as an active *trace* in Du Bois's discourse even though it now functions, as Jacques Derrida would say, "under erasure."[12] However, note how Appiah puts it when he argues that "substituting a sociohistorical conception of race for the biological one ... is simply to bury the biological conception below the surface, not to transcend it."[13] If true, this is a serious matter to which we should give urgent attention.

In a brief but bold conclusion, Appiah argues that the discursive or sociohistorical turn is doomed to fail since it cannot free itself of the biological trace that adheres to the concept of race when such a move is performed "under Saussurean hegemony."[14] The crucial question at issue here is whether we have too easily come to think of *meaning* in a post-Saussurean manner as primarily a linguistic phenomenon, as something constituted by systems of difference that are purely internal to the formally structured rules of *langue,* the abstract ordering principles of language that Saussure distinguished from speech acts, or *parole.* If the problem amounts to a semiotic fall from grace, then the Saussureans must suppose that race is, as Appiah puts it, "like all other concepts, constructed by metaphor and metonymy; it stands in, metonymically, for the Other; it bears the weight, metaphorically, of other kinds of difference." For Appiah, even if the concept of race *is* a "structure of oppositions," then it is one "whose realization is, at best, problematic, and at worst, impossible," for the question is: what is the actual entity to which it refers? In response to this dilemma he concludes that "the truth is that there are no races: there is nothing in the world that can do all we ask 'race' to do for us." He continues, "Where race works—in places where 'gross differences' of morphology are correlated with 'subtle differences' of temperament, belief, and intention—it works as an attempt at a metonym for culture; and it does so only at the price of biologizing what *is* culture, or ideology." Standing against the discursive turn, Appiah states, "What we miss through our obsession with the structure of relations of concepts is, simply, reality."[15] On this view, we should have the courage of our convictions and give race up altogether as a philosophically unacceptable way of talking.

Here, finally, at the end of a brilliant intervention, I find myself parting company with Appiah's argument. I have, of course, no commitment whatsoever to defending race as a concept, least of all in its genetic, biological, or so-called scientific form. Nevertheless, I do not understand what is meant by saying that racial discourse, when conceptualized as a "structure of oppositions," cannot be "realized." Does this mean the discursive turn with regard to race has no purchase on the real world, has no effects "out there" beyond what he calls the "text-world of the academy," because it is *only* language, nothing but discourse? That because we cannot find a scientific referent for racial difference, it does not exist as a sociohistorical fact? What exactly is the nature of Appiah's appeal to, "simply, reality" in light of his methodological preoccupation with a structure of relations analogous to *langue,* that is, language as a system of differences?

My argument is that this deconstructive move—counterposing the biological to the sociohistorical and, finding the biological-scientific conception of race unfounded and untenable, settling for the cultural and the hermeneutic—has one still unfinished turn to complete. Scholars in the academy, Appiah suggests, have been too reluctant to share with their fellow citizens their inescapable conclusion, which is to advocate the "repudiation of race as a term of difference."[16] If what he means by this is that race has no scientific foundations as an explanatory mechanism for accounting for social, cultural, economic, and cognitive differences between racially defined groups, then of course I agree. But we still have to explain why these racial classificatory systems persist, why so much of history has been organized within the shadow of their primordial binaries, and why, above all, everyday action and commonsense language and thought—as well as the larger structural systems of power that organize the distribution of wealth, resources, and knowledge differentially across societies and between groups—all continue to operate with this apparently weak, unsubstantiated, untenable, nearly but not quite erased "biological" trace. Simply put, we still have to account for why race is so tenacious in human history, so impossible to dislodge.

Appiah undertakes his deconstruction like a true philosopher when he argues we should be concerned not just with "the meaning of race" but with "the truth of it."[17] To which one can only respond: since when has the discourse of race (or, indeed, of sex and gender, whose similarities Appiah notes in this respect), let alone its real effects, been determined by "the truth" in this absolute sense? What I think is still missing from this dismantling of our problem is an account of how race works *discursively,* and of the centrality of its status as a signifier to its deadly operations in the world and to its real effects. These are not the operations of race as evolutionary biology or modern genetics understand it, but how it is understood precisely in terms of metaphor and metonymy, which Appiah seems to dismiss but which are the terms of what I am calling its signifying and discursive operation within our various systems of meaning.

I sense three kinds of reservation to the argument I am advancing, which I want to bring right out into the open at this point. They are related kinds of objection, on a sliding scale of importance. The first is the *philosophical* objection, which Appiah himself advances. On this view, analyzing the structure of oppositions that define a concept is a diverting linguistic game, but if the concept—signifier and signified—has no scientific referent in the real world, then the whole game collapses into a sort of trivial semiotic pursuit. The second objection is *political* and *historical* and is shadowed in Appiah's ominous reference to, "simply, reality." Does not all this talk of conceptual distinctions and binary oppositions pale into insignificance beside the horrendous consequences, the human havoc, that racism in action has wrought on the lives of millions of people across the centuries who frankly could not care less about what Saussure, Foucault, or Derrida has to say? This shades into a third objection, which we may call *evidential* or *experiential*. What is all this talk about whether or not race really exists when we only have to use the evidence of our own eyes to *see* the inscription of racial difference in the skin color, hair, and bones—in the physiology, morphology, and melanin composition— of diverse human groups who behave, on the basis of these differences, in all too predictable ways toward one another?

Against the commonsense obviousness of all those points, I do nevertheless want to advance the scandalous argument that, socially, historically, and politically, race is a discourse; that it operates like a language, like a sliding signifier; that its signifiers reference not genetically established facts but the systems of meaning that have come to be fixed in the classifications of culture; and that those meanings have real effects not because of some truth that inheres in their scientific classification but because of the will to power and the regime of truth that are instituted in the shifting relations of discourse that such meanings establish with our concepts and ideas in the signifying field.[18] This will to truth of the idea of race achieves its effects through the ways in which discursive systems organize and regulate the social practices of men and women in their daily interactions with one another. This is, in my view, precisely the theoretical purchase that the concept of discourse has over that awkward binary that counterposes ideology and practice. Far from signaling just talk, as if to say we are dealing with nothing but language, the term "discourse" suggests exactly the breaking down of the distinction between these two levels of "pure ideas" and "brute practice" in favor of the insistence that all human, social, and cultural practices are always both, that is they are always *discursive practices.* And this means we must be cautious before too hastily trying to distinguish the discursive from the extradiscursive.

To put it crudely, racial discourses constitute one of the great, persistent classificatory systems of human culture, and as such, they are also always discursive systems—systems for the representation of, and the organization of practices around, one of the great facts about human society, namely, the fact of difference. This is to understand race as a "trope of ultimate, irreducible difference between cultures," as Gates put it in his introduction to *"Race," Writing, and*

Difference. Analytically, we may be able to understand how such systems operate in formal terms, as a structure or system of similarities and differences within which race is a figure or trope that produces meanings. But what matters historically is that these meanings then organize and are inscribed within the practices and operations of *relations of power* between groups. This is to view such meanings not merely as textual or linguistic but as discursive systems, that is to say, systems where the signifying relations of similarity and difference depend not on some one-to-one relationship of race with a given order of "real" distinctions—biological or physical—out there in the world but on the ways in which the enormous spectrum of (apparently randomly distributed) differences that exist in the material world are constructed as a system of differentiations in language and thus *made meaningful,* constituting a system of intelligibility for human understanding, knowledge, and everyday practice. Such meanings of "race" are discursive in terms of the way they are referenced within the play of similarity and difference by which all systems of discourse construct human action as meaningful conduct. These meanings are also discursive, in my usage, because the interplay between the representation of difference, the production of knowledge, and the inscription of power on the body is a threefold relationship that is critical to the production of race. Hence not only do I use *discursive* here to mark the transition, theoretically, from a formal, linguistic, and textual understanding of difference, which we find addressed to questions of language in Saussure, Claude Lévi-Strauss, and structuralism, toward the models put forward by Foucault, Derrida, and the postcolonial theorists of the dialogics of otherness, but I also use *discursive* to expand on the Foucauldian syllogism *power-knowledge*, so as to include what I believe is always its necessary but silent third term, which gives us *power-knowledge-difference*.

Since we are concerned not with an abstract theoretical critique but with an attempt to unlock the secrets of the functioning in modern history of racial systems of classification and their all-too-real effects, the question of how discursive systems are said to reference the real world is of central importance, especially because this is where the question of scientific validity—or, as Appiah puts it, "not only the meaning but the truth" of racial discourse—and thus the troubling question of the biological in Du Bois's "grosser physical differences of color, hair and bone" return to haunt our argument.

Broadly speaking, there are three basic options available to us here. First, we can hold that differences of a genetic, biological, or physical nature really do exist and provide the basis for classifying the human race into families according to phenotypical and other characteristics, and that once they can be proved to exist scientifically, they can be accurately represented in the discursive system. If not, then the discourse has no foundation in reality and such classificatory systems are, as Gates puts it, "arbitrary constructs, not aspects of reality." Hence the concept of race must be "pseudo-scientific," for when "we carelessly use language in such a way as to *will* this sense of *natural* difference into our formulations," we are engaged in "a pernicious use of language."[19]

Second, we can hold to the purely linguistic-textual position. Here race is a self-referential, autonomous belief system in that it cannot be tested in any way against the reality of the world of human diversity, since it exists only in discourse. If there is nothing outside the text, then race exists only within the "systems of differences purely internal to our endlessly structured *langues,*" as Appiah put it in his criticism of those who proceed "under Saussurean hegemony." The third position—and the one to which I subscribe—

is that of course there are indeed material differences of all sorts in the world. There is no reason to deny this reality. However, it is only when these differences have been organized within discourse, as a system of marked differentiations, that the resulting categories can be said to acquire meaning, become a factor in human culture, regulate conduct, and have real effects on everyday social practices.

From this third position the questions remains: how we can identify such meaningful differences without language? There is no way of knowing, and certainly no way of proving, that the differences we call race already exist in nature, since how do we know this is what we should call them except as they have been constructed through discourse? By the same token, there is no ground on which we can absolutely deny their materiality except through the distinction between what is and what is not in language, even though such a distinction itself requires and presupposes language. As Judith Butler succinctly puts it,

> To "refer" naively or directly to such an extra-discursive object will always require the prior delimitation of the extra-discursive. And insofar as the extra-discursive is delimited, it is formed by the very discourse from which it seeks

to free itself. This delimitation, which often is enacted as an untheorized presupposition in any act of description, marks a boundary that includes and excludes, that decides, as it were, what will and will not be the stuff of the object to which we then refer.[20]

This suggests that what is "natural" to the bodies we perceive as racial is, in fact, a material surface on which language makes its inscriptive marks of intelligibility, thereby rendering it knowable in racialized terms precisely because human variations have already been taken up into and represented within an overall system of signification. Butler, however, criticizes this soft version in which the natural is "that which is 'before' intelligibility," arguing that it misses the point that nature always has a history.[21] The relevant parts of the body taken up into racial discourse form an enormously selective set, leaving out many other parts of the body that are specified and foregrounded in other discourses of difference, such as gender. It is thus increasingly difficult to identify what this presocial, prediscursive, purely natural and material, unraced body would be like, where we could find it, and how we could identify it outside the play of the discursive. It does not follow, however, that by taking up the discursive position we abolish nature; we are saying only that nature cannot be taken as the prediscursive "origin" of racial discourses or as the source of their foundational truth.

What we know about the social world—with knowledge now as the key term in our power-knowledge-difference equation—matters. But such knowledge is not independently accessible in any form in which it is foundational to the racializing discourses of difference, and thus it cannot be used as a way of actually adjudicating contested claims about race, because such knowledge *is itself* discursively organized and produced. Gates reminds us how Nancy Stepan, in her remarkable 1982 book *The Idea of Race in Science,* has shown that the tropes and metaphors of race "have sought a universal and transcendent sanction in biological science," and that Western thinkers and writers "have tried to mystify these rhetorical figures of race, to make them natural, absolute, essential."[22] This is, of course, true, but successive failures to find a foundational basis in science have not prevented successive generations from having another shot at it. Hence I would argue that in fully completing the turn toward a discursive conception of race, what is at stake is not whether there is some ultimate or final truth about the meaning of race to be found in the knowledge produced by science, but that our object of investigation shifts to examine the historical forms of knowledge that produce the intelligibility of race. And this is to say that since the Renaissance at least, and especially since the Enlightenment, it is Science, with a capital *S*, that bears the imperatives of the will to truth about the human species, its orderings and classifications, its varieties and distinctions, and its relations of super- and subordination.

Histories of Difference

Racial classification systems themselves have a history, and their modern history seems to emerge where the peoples of Europe first encounter, and have to make sense of, the peoples and cultures of the New World, and when the process of imperial expansion begins as Europe breaks out from its physical and conceptual confinement at the end of the Middle Ages. This is the historical moment when what Mary Louise Pratt has called the great "Euro-imperial adventure" begins, which is also the great Euro-imperial encounter with difference.[23] When Europeans of the Old World first encountered the peoples and cultures of the New World in the 1400s, they put to themselves a great question: not "Are you not a son and a brother, are you not a daughter and a sister?"—which comes much later, with the moment of antislavery in the 1700s—but rather "Are these true men? Do they belong to the same species as us? Or are they born of another creation?" This was the question Juan Ginés de Sepúlveda debated with Bartolomé de Las Casas before the Holy Roman Emperor at Valladolid in 1550. This is the form in which the question of racial difference was first framed in modern Western discourse. Here, and for several centuries, it was religion—not science—that stood as the guarantor of "truth." One might say it was religion that stood where science was destined to stand as it formed the discursive foundation on which Europeans strove so hard—and failed—to ground the representation of human difference and diversity in "truth."

For centuries the struggle was to establish a line of binary distinction in the classificatory system between two mutually exclusive creations of the human race. It was only with the Enlightenment—under whose panoptic, universalist eye all gradations of human difference came to be represented in the discourse of natural philosophy as parts of a single system—that, as it were, the discursive mark of difference shifts to a new position: not between two mutually exclusive species but between differential levels and grades of "civilization" and "barbarism" within one single system. This is a new type of binary structure of representation, between the West and its others, which requires a more exquisitely differentiated and continuously sustained marking of various grades, degrees, and levels within an overall system of human difference. As Edmund Burke put it when he wrote to William Robertson on June 9, 1777, addressing the way the entire globe was now at last under the eye of the Western Enlightenment philosopher, who saw the world *sub specie aeternitatis*:

> We need no longer go to History to trace it [the knowledge of human nature] in all its stages and periods . . . now the Great map of mankind is unrolled at once, and there is no state or Gradation of barbarism, and no mode of refinement we have not at the same instant under our View. The very different Civility of Europe and China; the barbarism of Persia and Abyssinia; the erratic manners of Tartary, and of Arabia. The Savage state of North America and of New Zealand.[24]

My point, then, is that what matters is not science per se but rather whatever is the overarching discourse that grounds the "truth" about human culture, the

relations between "nature" and "culture," and the puzzling facts of human diversity. I am not suggesting
anything as far-fetched as saying that science cannot
give us knowledge of the physical material world.
Nothing I am saying should be construed as arguing
that there are no physiological, morphological, or
genetic differences among groups of people in the
world. But my question is this: what do these differences *mean?* Can they explain, or ground foundationally in some notion of truth, the discrepancies
of power and wealth, of behavior and dispensation, of
culture, language, and so on, which constitute the
real objects that racialized discourse has referred to
throughout modern history?

What is at issue here is the foundation of truth
that science has performed within modern cultural
systems from the eighteenth century onward. In
talking about the cultural and discursive effects of
science as a regime of truth, I am suggesting that the
entire function of science in the language of race,
like that of religion before it, has been to provide exactly the certainty and guarantee of absolute knowledge that no other system of knowledge has been
able to provide. What matters about science or religion is not that either one contains the actual truth
about difference, but that each functions *foundation-*

ally in the discourse of race to fix and secure what cannot be finally fixed and secured. What we hear in Burke's words is the language of natural philosophy that seeks to warrant and guarantee in nature the "truth" of the differences—social, cultural, economic, political—that were being discursively constructed within a new historical regime whose foundations in the 1700s were provided by science. The point is not that each regime that grounds the "truth" shows how racial difference actually arises in nature, but rather that each regime of truth *makes difference function discursively.* Indeed, by making difference intelligible in this way, each regime marks out human differences within culture in a way that corresponds exactly to how difference is understood to function in nature, that is, "naturally," such that the differences represented in the discourse of race are put beyond the capacity of culture and history to rework or reconstruct them.

The work science has performed in the eighteenth century and onward is to establish what Ernesto Laclau calls a "chain of equivalences" between nature and culture that thus makes race function discursively as a system of representation.[25] Laclau has convincingly argued that central to the construction of hegemony—the form of power that wants to win consent to its "truth"—is the discursive formation of chains of equivalence between signifying elements that have no necessary or part-for-part correspondence between them. It is this condensation effect, he argues, in his example of the Moral Majority's discourse, that allows "the family," for instance, to become an organic element in the otherwise conflicting discourse about "market forces," thereby producing what is in fact an *articulation* among discourses that have no necessary correspondence but which come to be represented discursively as a naturalized equivalence such that one can "read off" the one, nature, from its counterpart in the other, culture. What we are looking at is not, in effect, nature, but what Karl Marx, in the discussion of ideology that has been least attended to of late but which is of enduring interest, described as the "naturalization effect" that arises when discourses about culture and history, which are variable across space, time, and circumstances—and which, because they are sociohistorically variable, are thus amenable to change—come to represent themselves as warranted, guaranteed in place, and hence permanent, fixed, unmovable, and transhistorical by virtue of nature.[26] It is not that physical differences among humans are or are not scientifically explicable but that their cultural meaning has to be discursively constructed "scientifically" because science's appeal to nature is, in our modern era, the foundational language in which truth claims can be advanced, explained, and fixed beyond human interventions. I am tempted to quote from Marx's much-abjected *The German Ideology,* but I will turn instead to Roland Barthes's example, in *Mythologies,* of the image of a black soldier in his army uniform saluting the French tricolor, from the cover of *Paris-Match* in the 1950s, about which Barthes says:

> Myth hides nothing and flaunts nothing: it distorts; myth is neither a lie nor a confession; it is an inflection . . . [D]riven to having either to unveil or to liquidate the concept, it will *naturalize it.* We reach here the very principle of myth: it transforms history into nature . . . [E]verything happens as if the picture *naturally* conjured up the concept, as if the signifier *gave a foundation* to the signified . . . [M]yth is speech justified *in excess.*[27]

This approach gives us one reason to understand why, it seems to me, the biological trace is unlikely to disappear entirely from the discourses of racial difference even though the foundational marking of phenotype and genetics was radically weakened with the discrediting of scientific definitions of race after World War II. So long as the naturalizing, essentializing, and dehistoricizing function remains with science in general, the appeal to nature made whenever race is our subject of discussion has as its basis the operation of power-knowledge-difference, whose discursive functioning has to be examined historically rather than formally.

However, this is not the only reason the biological, while functioning "under erasure," continues to be so necessary to, and so difficult to eliminate from, the discourses of racial difference. What Du Bois started with, and what Appiah argues Du Bois could not quite dissociate himself from—notwithstanding the fluctuations and dissonances it produced in his own discourse on the subject—was precisely "the grosser physical differences of color, hair and bone," which, despite the fact that they remain anomalous to actual populations and "transcend scientific definition," are what finally come to underpin the division of the great families of human beings into races in our commonsense understanding of the world.

Now, the central fact about these "grosser physical differences" is not that they are correlated with genetic differentiation, as Appiah convincingly shows, but that they matter because they are, as Du Bois says, "*clearly defined to the eye*," and I add this emphasis since it applies not only to the eye of the historian and the sociologist but to the eye of everybody. Such differences are absolutely, obviously, and incontrovertibly the *evidence* of something meaningful that is perceptible to the untutored, unscientific eye. They are differences that, in this sense, come to be put beyond dispute as brute physical-biological facts about "race" because of their existence in the field of vision. Seeing is believing, as the commonsense saying has it. This obviousness of race is the experiential bedrock upon which the sociocultural and historical definitions so often flounder. As you know, Frantz Fanon, in his superb work on the psychic mechanisms of racism, *Black Skin, White Masks,* was transfixed by the inscription of racial difference on the black body, such that his attention was riveted on what he called the "dark and unarguable" evidence of the fact of blackness, which made him the slave "not of the 'idea' that others have of me but of my own appearance."[28] What Fanon argues is that the bodily self-image or corporeal schema, which is so critical for the foundation of self-identity and subjectivity because "it is . . . a definitive structuring of the self and of the world" and "creates a real dialectic between my body and the world," is shattered and destroyed

by the racializing look that comes from the place of
the white other—"Look, a Negro! . . . Mama, see the
Negro. I'm frightened."[29] In place of the corporeal
schema, it is this look that conveys the stereotypical
imago of the black person that is, "woven out of a
thousand details, anecdotes, stories." From this moment, "I am fixed," Fanon says, as his blackness is
"sealed into that crushing objecthood," "overdetermined from without," when "the movements, the at-
titudes, the glances of the other fixed me there, in the
sense in which a chemical solution is fixed by a dye,"
and from which "now the fragments have been put
back together again by another self."[30] This splitting
into thinghood, the fixing of the black person in the
white mask as a result of the look, is achieved by what
Fanon eloquently calls the process of *epidermalization*—the inscription of racial difference on the skin.
And it is exactly this racial-epidermal schema that is
at issue in Du Bois's "color, hair and bone."

Epidermalization fixes the "truth" of racial difference in its *bodily inscription,* and this makes of the
black body itself, and its physiological characteristics,
the terminal point of the will to truth or regime of
truth regarding race, which in turn implies that the
black body is a sort of transcendental signifier, something capable of fixing the meaning of race *tout court.*
And yet even here, I want to argue, the play of signi-

fiers, of sliding signifiers, is at work. For what gives rise to these evidentiary and highly visible signs of racial difference—fuzzy hair, big noses, thick lips, large buttocks, and, as the French writer Michel Cournot, quoted by Fanon, delicately put it, penises that "would fill a cathedral"[31]—and produces them as meaningful, what epidermalizes them, is something *that cannot be seen:* the genetic codes. So what precisely tends to fix race in its obviousness and visibility—in physical characteristics of "color, hair and bone"—are themselves nothing but the signifiers of an invisible code that writes difference upon the black body. These physical features are therefore the markers of racial difference at the level of appearances, which makes them signs of a code that itself cannot be directly accessed except by science. What looks literally as if it fixes race in all its materiality—the obvious visibility of black bodies—is actually functioning as a set of signifiers that direct us to *read* the bodily inscription of racial difference and thus render it intelligible. How, then, do these signifiers work discursively? It is by allowing us to read off one set of signifiers in nature along its chain of equivalences in culture, which is to say that these signifiers of epidermalization work precisely by metaphor and metonymy.

The fixing of difference, which has to secure a relationship of signifier to signified at one point in the

chain, slides along the chain of equivalences, as
Laclau calls them, to metaphorically anchor all the
other binaries of difference correspondingly. What is
held to be "obvious" at the commonsense level of appearances is thus "true" back down the chain at the
level of the genetic, which is the domain of science
and which concerns something that can be seen only
in its effects, namely, the bodily differences of "color,
hair and bone." But simultaneously these physical
signifiers can also be metonymically displaced further
up the signifying chain, where they are correspondingly
read as "true" when it comes to differences of culture,
intellectual and cognitive capacity, emotional temperament, and social accomplishment, and ultimately for
registering degrees of "civilization" and "barbarism,"
which, since the Enlightenment, is what racial classification has been all about. On this account, it is not
quite, as Appiah puts it, that the language of race bi-
ologizes culture. Rather, the operations of the sliding
signifier work to suture and secure the meaningful-
ness of cultural difference through the way in which
the biological and the physiological come to function discursively in the signifying field. My argument requires that we understand race as a floating
signifier, and that we must approach racial classification systems as discursive operations of meaning if

we are to unpack their functioning socially, historically, and politically.

If I am right about the way race functions discursively, then the question of what can or cannot be
shown to be "true" in scientific terms at the biological level has, in fact, only a very indirect bearing on
how racial discourses work in the world in sociohistorical terms. To put it the other way round, one
might say that the indirect bearing of science on the
sociohistorical functioning of race also relates to how
easy or difficult it might be—having made the decisive move to reject the biological-physiological as an
adequate explanation of cultural difference—to ex-
punge its discursive traces from the system. Let us
recall that it was precisely to prevent this metonymic
slide from performing its deadly work in the world
that Du Bois appeared to change his mind when, in
contrast to his 1897 position, he wrote in *The Crisis* in
1911 that "it is not legitimate to argue from differences in physical characteristics to differences in
mental characteristics," and that "the civilization of
a people or race at any particular moment of time offers no index to its innate or inherited capacities."[32]

The problem is that in moving to a sociohistorical
and civilizational, rather than biologistic, definition
of race, Du Bois still seems to want to find at the

social, historical, and cultural levels something that would define as a distinct *racial essence* that which he could not find at the level of biological-genetic differences. The idea that this essential element is spiritual, not physical, and that it is to be discovered in the fact that each race has "its particular message, its particular ideal," which will make its unique contribution to the "perfection of human life," as he had put it in 1897, is a far more dignified solution to the problem than the available alternatives, but it does not seem to me, in the end, to be acceptable either.[33] The intervention of the black peoples in modern history and their transformation of systems of racial oppression constitute a unique contribution to world civilization, with effects that could not have been realized in any other way. But it does not seem helpful to understand this as the process of a race making its essential message, its "Negro message," heard, for there is more than a trace of Du Bois's residual Hegelianism in such a teleological conception. I prefer his *Dusk of Dawn* formulation, where Du Bois's conception of a people who suffered a common disaster, who share a common history, who have one long memory, which is the social heritage of slavery, and who are marked by color as a "badge," culminates in this last emphasis on rereading race as a sign, a marker of difference that carries sociohistorical and cultural meaning. Even though it cannot do the work Du Bois wishes it to do—ground a set of differences among races or provide the basis for the tie he feels with Africa—the *Dusk of Dawn* formulation does move the argument decisively toward the sociohistorical and the cultural. The problem, then, is that once we are on this terrain and have renounced the function of the biological to fix the truth or meaning of race, we are thus in the uncertain terrain of open-ended, discursive systems where *difference,* among the signifiers of race, begins its discursive slide with a vengeance.

As I come toward conclusion, I need to stress that it is not that the biological definition of race is pure falsification, a mystification, an ideological illusion we can do away with by referring it to some other, higher, scientific truth. It is not that there are no biological characteristics among different populations, and it certainly is not that, if "race" is used loosely enough, we cannot identify some of the "grosser physical differences of color, hair and bone" to which the term refers. Rather, the issue is that the biological-physiological level *can never do what it claims in the discourse to do:* it cannot establish permanent differences among diverse families of races; it cannot give these cultural, social, economic, and historical differences a guaranteed basis of inheritance in genetic distinctions; and it cannot fix, for either negative or positive purposes, the cultural, cognitive, emotional, and other social characteristics of the populations to which it refers. However, because such differences, however "gross" in scientific terms, exist, they can be given a meaning—they can be *constructed and reconstructed as discursive objects*. As such, they can be used to perform all kinds of discursive work. Such constructions of difference can produce certain kinds of knowledge about the world, including the production of racializing knowledge of an obvious, taken-for-granted, commonsense kind, which is the most dangerous of all forms of knowledge because it is the most unconscious. This racialized knowledge about difference has the power to organize everyday conduct as well as the various practices of groups toward one another, and such knowledges enter deeply into, and profoundly disfigure, the culture of the societies in which they are operative over long periods.

Transcoding the Signifier

In one sense, then, Appiah is right, for on the one hand race cannot perform the work—provide the truth, fix the meaning of cultural differences beyond any shadow of a doubt—that the defenders and opponents of racial oppression want it to do when they draw on its great classificatory systems and taxonomies to explain or organize their practice. But, on the other hand, in the discursive sense as I have tried to describe it, the chain of equivalences that race *makes possible* between genetic, physical, social, and cultural difference does actually exist. Not only does this chain of equivalences remain extensively present in the world, in the meanings we use to make sense of social life and social practices everywhere, but also, even though it is "only a discourse," it has for that very reason a reality because it has racial effects— material effects in how power and resources are distributed, symbolic effects in how groups are ranked relationally to one another, psychic effects that form the interior space of existence of every subject constructed by it and caught up in the play of its signifiers.

Indeed, I believe that it is precisely *because* of its historical-discursive effects that we need to take account of the chain of equivalences made possible by race. Though in one sense it is only one of the many discourses of cultural difference in our modern history, it has a distinctiveness, a specificity, that arises because it is the one that, however unscientifically, continues to operate using the physical markers of difference *on the body* as the privileged signifiers of its regime of truth. In this respect—despite the many other reasons why antiracists have sometimes been at considerable pains to deny the similarities—it is the discourse of difference closest to that of sexual difference, which also "reads" the evidence of the body discursively, trying to fix social and cultural meanings biologically, and thereby acquiring something of the same pervasive obviousness as race within "the field of vision," as Jacqueline Rose puts it.[34] Sigmund Freud remarked in his important paper "Some Psychical Consequences of the Anatomical Distinction between the Sexes" that when the little girl sees the penis of her male counterpart, "she makes her judgement and her decision in a flash. She has seen it and knows that she is without it and wants to have it."[35] One could say the same of the little child in Fanon's *Black Skin, White Masks* who cries out, "Look, a Negro! . . . Mama, see the Negro. I'm frightened." In both instances it is not the anatomical or epidermal schema that matters in the formation of subjective identity, or in the regulatory effects of the discursive practices of gender and race; rather, what matters is the fact that these bodily attributes are taken up into discourse, where they then become the *objects* of psychic fantasy in our subjective lives as in our institutional lives and everyday social practices.

Of course, the discourse of racism operates in a world of Manichean opposites—them and us, primitive and civilized, light and dark—which creates a seductive black-and-white symbolic universe. But after a while, its reductive simplicity itself becomes problematic because of its banality: once you have unpacked its simplistic logic, you can struggle against it, but can you really spend a lifetime studying it? In fact, I believe we are only at the beginning of understanding the complexity of such structures and mechanisms once we move decisively and irrevocably from a biogenetically secured conception of race to a discursive-historical one. That is to say, racism's apparent simplicities and rigidities are precisely what is symptomatically important about it. *Racism's rigidity is the clue to its complexity.* Its capacity to punctuate the complex cultural and historical world into two great opposites masks the deep ambivalences of feeling, attitude, belief, and worldview that always refuse to be neatly stabilized and fixed. The great binary divisions of racial discourse as a structure of knowledge and representation can, it seems to me, also be understood as a deep system of defense. Such binaries are the outworks and trenches, the defensive positions around something—the fully historicized configurations of cultural difference—that refuses to be tamed and contained by that system of representation. All the symbolic and narrative energy, all the discursive work, that goes into keeping the racial signifier afloat is directed toward securing us "over here" and them "over there," constantly striving to fix each identity into its appointed species place. But all such efforts would not be necessary were it not for the tendency that culture always shows, as a structure of similarities and differences that is open to the "play" of signification, the "play" of history: the tendency for all signifiers to slip and slide out of place. Racism's simplifications, which endeavor to polarize and separate, mask how deeply our histories and cultures have always intertwined and interpenetrated, how absolutely necessary the other is to our own sense of identity. The operation of the systems I have been tracking in this lecture all work to mask the extent to which identity is an open and differential phenomenon, dependent on the frontier effects of discursive markers to fix the difference between the "inside" and the constitutive "outside," which keep slipping into each other. As Butler reminds us, it is precisely in order to find stability in the face of such slipping and sliding of the signifier that every identity is also an expulsion, to the constitutive outside, of those who come to be marked as other.[36]

With Fanon we come to see that, in addition to the symbolic violence and aggression that inform the look from the other—which has the coercive force that is so characteristic of racial stereotyping, of projection, of defense, of denial and disavowal—we must also understand the discursive work that has to be carried out in the symbolic economy of a culture in order to control and contain the danger, the threat, the fear, and the phobia that the play of difference itself represents. What Fanon draws our attention to is not the fixed difference of bodies or identities that remain immured in their otherness but the slippery, sliding system of similarities and differences that *is* the fully historicized conception of culture. We thus come to understand the exercise of discursive power that is required to symbolically expel difference to the far side of the universe—and the surreptitious return whereby that which has been expelled keeps coming back home to trouble the dreams of the sleeper with the terrifying internal fears, the nightmares, of having to live with difference.

The very binary narrative form that seeks to contain the sliding of the racial signifier always has, despite the real effects of violence and aggression implicit in racist representation, a double-sided and deeply ambivalent character. We see that side by side with the dependent, childlike, vicious, barbaric, primitive, and treacherous narratives of race produced by the system of representation is the powerful nostalgia that is never far away, inscribing the secret desire of so-called civilized societies for the erotic power of the body, for an emotional register of expressivity, for an eloquent endurance of suffering, for a rhythmic force—for some essential difference—that has apparently been lost to the so-called civilized world. The double inscription of racial discourse—the violence of racism that is structured around loss, the desire for the other that is inextricably coupled to its obliteration—means that the discursive structures we are dealing with are never capable of speaking alone, one without the other, for both are equally an essentializing narrative projection from the same binary system.

It is all the more striking and incongruous, then, that the politics of opposition to racist systems of classification so often operates in exactly the same way discursively as the systems it contests: through an essentialized conception of race. Antiracism inverts the position of all the terms in the discursive system. Hence, what for racists is the incontrovertible evidence that blacks cannot overcome their negative characteristics because they are fixed genetically and biologically by race is held by antiracist movements everywhere to be precisely the features of a racial essence that secures a positive, special, privileged or even exceptional position for blacks in human history and which is transmitted by the biological and genetic inheritance of which the "grosser physical differences" are the sign and guarantee. The value of each of the signifiers in the discursive system has been reversed, from negative to positive, but paradoxically the paradigm remains the same: cultural, historical, and political characteristics remain fixed and guaranteed by the biological and the genetic, only each attribute now functions as the mirror image, with its racial essence reversed, of the other in the opposing discourse. We are left with the same paradigm standing on its head. My description here is far from simply a theoretical or theoreticist critique, as if the politics of the movements against racial oppression could be guaranteed by being subject to a theoretically correct reclassification. The problem, rather, is that grounding a political movement and a cultural politics in an essentialist racial trope, from either end of the political spectrum, has real, very serious, and profound political effects that cannot be left unexamined.

I have tried elsewhere to spell out some of the implications of this problem in a phrase that has since acquired a certain notoriety—"the end of the essential black subject." I want to now say with increased emphasis that, in my view, breaking free from a biologistic conception of race, which is operative even when, as is the case in Britain today, racial discourse appears to have decisively moved to a form of cultural racism, entails and indeed requires "the end of the innocent notion of the essential black subject." I have tried to summarize this in the following way:

> What is at issue here is the recognition of the extraordinary diversity of subjective positions, social experiences, and cultural identities which compose the category "black"; that is, the recognition that "black" is essentially a politically and culturally *constructed* category, which cannot be grounded in a set of fixed transcultural or transcendental racial categories and which therefore has no guarantees in Nature. . . . This inevitably entails a weakening or fading of the notion that "race" or some composite notion of "race" around the term "black" will either guarantee the effectivity of any cultural practice or determine in any final sense its aesthetic

value.... Once you enter the politics of the end of the essential black subject you are plunged headlong into the maelstrom of a continuously contingent, unguaranteed, political argument and debate: a critical politics, a politics of criticism.[37]

To move decisively toward a rigorously sociohistorical, cultural, and discursive conception of the politics of race is not in any way to deny the specificity of the shared experiences of oppression, exploitation, and marginalization that are structured on racial grounds. Nor is it in any sense to underplay the shaping of black historical experiences through the functioning of the racial signifier, the cultural traditions that have persisted, evolved, and been transferred through collective historical experience. All this is the common legacy of struggle and resistance that, as Du Bois put it, is the "social heritage of slavery," alongside the distinctive forms of life shaped by the subjection to a "common disaster," and the depth and intensity with which black expressive cultures have been formed by what he called "one long memory." But to move toward a discursive conception of the politics of race is, I would emphasize, to recognize that every cultural tradition is a *reworking*, a production *anew,* a transformation, a remaking of identity that is specific to time, place, and circumstance and thus *cannot* simply be the persistent, unchanging preservation and replication across time, space, and history of some essential, originary, naturalized "same." What follows from the discursive approach I have put forward here is that specificity and transformation—the transcoding, reconstruction, and rearticulation of signifying elements—*are* exactly the historical and political "work" that culture does.

Since, in this discursive conception of the politics of race, meaning is everything, we can say that although its movements are not random or infinitely variable, there is no escaping from the porous, permeable character of culture's formations, which results in the heteroglossia of culture, the multiple repertoires on which it draws, and the new combinations it is constantly making. There is no escape from what Mikhail Bakhtin would call the "multiaccentuality" of racial meaning, no way of preventing culture from slipping and sliding within the indeterminate semiosis of meaning; hence there is *no way of limiting or trying to fix the varieties of subjects that black people will become.*[38] The way in which the discursive structures of a culture become permeable, reconstitutable, and thus "historical" in the best and only sense of the word means that black identities are incapable of being harnessed to a mere repetition of their origins, however those origins may be construed, for the multiaccentuality of race as a sliding signifier means there is no way to limit the varieties of identity that the black experience will come to include.

Is race, then, nothing more or less than a sliding signifier? Something that appears in the racialized system of representation as the site of a set of discursive operations that matter only because they constitute a particular regime of truth that organizes social practices? Does the whole horrendous experience of race in the modern world come down to nothing more or less than a metaphor or a metonym of cultural difference, which is merely one among many of the discourses of cultural difference operating in our world? If so, why don't we simply give up the habit, like giving up smoking? There is a perfectly good word for cultural differences between groups, *ethnicity*, so why don't we simply dissolve what we call race into it? I turn to this question, trying to unsettle the concept of ethnicity as I have done that of race, in my second lecture.

2

ETHNICITY AND DIFFERENCE
IN GLOBAL TIMES

SINCE THE CONCEPT of "race" in racial discourse functions, as Anthony Appiah put it, as a "metonym for culture," should we not dispense with the problematic trappings introduced by the term's references to the biological and take the plunge—take culture seriously—so as to enter irrevocably into thinking about race in terms of "communities of meaning, shading variously into each another in the rich structure of the social world, [that] is the province not of biology but of hermeneutic understanding"?[1] But then again, is race after all, as the contemporary orthodoxy would have it, simply defined by culture alone?

I have tried to argue that we cannot get rid of the biological trace and eliminate the specificity of the racialized discourse just like that. This is not because race can do what those (on either side of the political spectrum) who regularly display it in its biological or genetic form think it can do, and it is not because the biological-genetic could ever establish the foundational truth claims of racial discourse. It is because racial discourse is not a form of truth in any case, but rather a "regime of truth," as I have framed this term in my first lecture. The biological-genetic element functions to fix difference discursively all along the chain of equivalences in the racial system of representation. Thus, whatever its "truth" in terms of scientific validity, it is through its *discursive operations* that race gives meaning to the world, makes a certain kind of sense of the world, constructs an order of intelligibility, organizes human practices within its categories, and thus comes to acquire real effects. To grasp this discursive functioning is to understand race as a sliding signifier.

Such a view does not undermine the argument that racial discourse operates to mask what are sociohistorical and cultural differences. But one implication of my viewpoint is that with all of the discourses of difference we are really on the terrain of the making of meaningful distinctions, which has always to be seen as articulated with the operations of power—with the real and symbolic effects of subordination and subjectification—which, in turn, work to position all discursive systems within its symbolic boundaries.

Our concern is with discursively produced "frontier effects," as Ernesto Laclau and Chantal Mouffe call them: the game of the white West constructing and consolidating Western and white identities through the discursive inscription of otherness.[2] As I have argued, the production of the West's others was inaugurated with the onset of the Euro-imperial adventure, which makes it coterminous with modernity—and which, I suggested, shifted after the Enlightenment from the marking of differences *between* different human species to the marking of difference *within* one continuous human spectrum, in relation to which race provided the trope for the fundamental polarization of human societies, with their various gradations and variations, into "civilization" and "barbarism." The discourse of race, with its pathologization and fetishization of the other in bodily terms, is, from this perspective, a historically specific, particularly vicious and virulent manifestation within that larger discursive formation of cultural difference that we may call Eurocentrism or Western-centrism. To reframe race ontologically in this way is in no sense to dismiss or underplay its historical specificity or the disastrous historical consequences of its effects over the centuries. Quite the reverse. It is to take race seriously as a discursive system for the production of otherness—a cultural and historical system that operates in the signifying field—and to acknowledge its real and differential effects, thereby refusing its reduction to some biologically guaranteed transcultural or transhistorical notion of difference grounded in nature. However, to make this critical move is also to recognize that seeing race precisely as a variant in the discourses of cultural difference brings it, analytically and theoretically, into new relations with the other discursive formations of difference, the other sites of antagonism, which the play of power-knowledge-difference produces.

If cultural difference is the wider discursive formation we are talking about, then there is, as I have pointed out on previous occasions, a perfectly good term that references this distinctive area of difference—the shared languages, traditions, religious beliefs, cultural ideas, customs, and rituals that bind together particular groups—into which, perhaps, what we currently refer to by the term "race" should be theoretically subsumed.[3] This term is, of course, "ethnicity". Now, I am aware of the deeply problematic and highly charged significance ethnicity carries in the American context, where it is almost, though perhaps not quite, as much of a contested concept as race itself. Ethnicity has a very specific place in the history of the American nation, a society that, quite unlike Western European nation-states, has understood itself to be, from its modern inception, a society of immigrants, and thus a nation of varied and indeed socially hierarchical ethnicities. Since the great migrations of the latter half of the nineteenth century, the United States has had the notion of itself as an ethnic melting pot—one that simmers and occasionally boils over but which mostly cooks the different ingredients without completely dissolving them—as one of its primary foundational myths. America is "God's crucible," as the playwright Israel Zangwill put it, "where all the races of Europe are melting and reforming."[4] *E pluribus unum:* out of many, one people—or not, as Alexis de Tocqueville strongly suspected.[5] The United States, more than any other developed Western industrial society, has been transformed by great waves of migration—and it is now being transformed again, by a new wave of migration, at the end of the twentieth century. It is thus fitting that the country's official philosophy of itself as a nation—liberal pluralism—reflects the heterogeneous ethnic composition and ethnically shaped interests of its people. "Ethnicity," in this context, became a much-used and widely contested concept in

American social science in the 1960s and 1970s, although with the new wave of immigrants today, especially from Central and Latin America, the Caribbean, and Asia, the concept has returned in a troubling and troubled form to the contemporary political stage.

I want at this point to expand my frame of inquiry, however, and to leave to one side for a moment the rich complexity of America seen through the historical lens of ethnicity (which has been so penetratingly examined in the recent work of Werner Sollors, among others), so as to bring my focus onto this last moment—namely, the movement of people at the end of the twentieth century, the great planned and unplanned migrations of our current moment. Though they affect the United States in particular ways, these migrations are a global phenomenon of historic significance.[6] I want to take this globalizing dimension as the centerpiece of my reflections today and try to put the specificity of contemporary U.S. experiences in this wider, global context so that we may relate globalization to the dramatic and unexpected return of ethnicity to the late modern or postmodern stage. In this way, my aim is to see the question of ethnicity—alongside and in an uneasy and unresolved relationship to race, on the one hand, and to nation, on the other—as posing a key problem that radically unsettles all three terms. Posing the question in this way presents us with what I see as *the* problem of the twenty-first century—the problem of living with difference—in a manner that is not only analogous to the problem of the "color line" that W. E. B. Du Bois pointed to more than a hundred years ago but also a historically specific transformation of it.

The Return of Ethnicity

Even in our more recent, late modern, global context, where ethnicity has acquired a clearer reference than in its earlier manifestations to what Du Bois called the "color line"—"the darker races of men in relation to the lighter"—the relationship between race and ethnicity remains troubled and problematic.[7] Not only are actual relations between blacks and ethnic minorities in the United States (and increasingly in Europe, east and west) difficult socially and politically, a source of friction and trouble as often as they are a site of alliance and common cause, but, in addition, the historical specificities to which the two terms "race" and "ethnicity" refer are actually very different. Each term has highly distinct temporalities in relation to its effects, with race and its histories

being one of the central dynamics—a founding historical fact—of American society and history, while
ethnicity, especially in its multicultural sense, is of
more recent origin and plays very differently in U.S.
society as compared to Europe. The tension between
the two terms also gives rise to the widespread concern that, once again, the scale and enormity of racial oppression will be sidelined as it gets dispersed
into the more segmented and generalized spectrum
of differential incorporation and exclusion that is associated with ethnicity.

A debate with a direct bearing on this question of
how race and ethnicity have been staged in recent
times occurred in the United Kingdom in the
1970s at exactly that point when the illusion of a
melting pot or assimilationist conclusion to the
Afro-Caribbean and Asian migrations of the 1950s
and 1960s was finally abandoned, following the rise
of openly racist agitation on the streets of British
cities and the passage of clearly racialized immigra-
tion laws by the British Parliament. Let me pause at
this point to note that the end of the assimilationist
dream that marked the first stage of Afro-Caribbean
and Asian migration is a watershed moment with
global historical significance for the argument
I am advancing here. It is the turning point when

first-generation migrants to the postwar United Kingdom finally abandoned the liberal-assimilationist dream in the face of persistent racism because the price, in terms of self-denial and collective self-abjection—real and symbolic—was simply too high to pay. Gradually, the great well-intentioned, post-Enlightenment, liberal discourse of assimilation came to reveal its dark side: that we could all belong to one "family of man" provided *you* became more and more like *us*. Migrants began to insist on their rights to be citizens with equal entitlements within the political community while remaining cultur-ally different—black and proud of it. This shift oc-curred in the aftermath of decolonization and, at the same time, in the immediate wake of the black consciousness revolution of the 1960s American civil rights movement, which, I would argue, fractured the assimilationist dream in similar ways.

I want to suggest that this turning point, arising in the 1960s, not only is an important development of the struggles against racial oppression and disad-vantage that had been ongoing since colonization and slavery, but is also a major, ruptural moment of break and transformation. Hitherto, antiracial argu-ments had solidly located their claims on the basis of the humanistic universalism of the Enlightenment—

the Enlightenment's "light" side, if you like—which was the side of universal citizenship the Haitian Revolution had invoked in its opening moments in 1791 when it appealed for the abolition of slavery to France's National Assembly in the name of the universal rights of man. What was said, in effect, was, "We are black but we are human and therefore universal citizens too." Yet, as we know, what was implicit in the dusty answer the National Assembly returned to Toussaint L'Ouverture was the panoptic humanist universalism whereby the Western Enlightenment and its revolutionary thought were actually grounded in an assimilationist particularism: "Yes, you are black and human, but to be truly human you must become French and European, that is, you must become civilized, like us."

Bhikhu Parekh, in his 1994 article "Superior People," has given us a significant contribution to making visible this dire contradiction at the heart of Enlightenment and liberal thought, bringing out its dark side.[8] Catherine Hall, a feminist cultural historian working on gender, race, and ethnicity who happens to be my partner, also draws our attention to this point. Her work on the role Jamaica plays in the constitution and in the imaginary of a white English ethnicity in the nineteenth-century period after abolition argues that we cannot understand the complexity of the shifting markers of difference that define the racial discursive formation in this moment until we also understand the genuine specificity represented by the thought of liberal, pro-abolitionist Baptist missionaries, who played such a key part in trying to produce a respectable, Christian freed slave subject, and a respectable, Christian black family in the villages of post-abolition Jamaica. Such liberal thought among Baptist missionaries has had real, substantive effects, for example in the persistent strength of black Baptism in the religious life of contemporary Jamaica, and it represented an important difference from both the "species" racism of the white Jamaican plantocracy and what we would understand today as a genuinely liberatory black discourse of racial equality.[9]

Hence my tentative proposition is that whereas the argument between equality claimed on the basis of universality or sameness, on the one hand, and equality claimed on the basis of difference, on the other, had already surfaced in the early feminism of the late eighteenth century and reappeared with a vengeance with the rise of the contemporary women's movement after 1968, it was not until the watershed moment of the 1960s and 1970s that this internal argument between "equality" and "difference" came to be widely constructed in antiracist and anticolonial discourse. The political recognition, and the cultural celebration, of difference from this moment onward therefore marks a seismic discursive rupture for the embracing of difference, for the reconfiguration of cultural difference as a positive focus of identity and identification, and it subsequently comes to redefine the broad field of social antagonisms in contemporary politics at large. This moment signals the break with the discourse of Enlightenment universalism and liberal humanism upon which, up to that point, struggles of resistance had been predicated. Though the "equality" discourse of the Enlightenment continues to function discursively in all the struggles against the dialectics of otherness, it is seriously dislocated from this point onward and put permanently "under erasure" by the discourse of "difference," and as a result all the claims based on ascribed similarity or sameness are submitted to what Derrida calls the endless play of the "weave of differences."[10] At this point the discourses of antiracism begin to share a contiguous discursive space with other discourses of cultural difference, and we enter definitively into a new post-Enlightenment moment in the politics of cultural identity.

We can now try to relocate the question of how Afro-Caribbean and Asian migrants to the United Kingdom in the 1950s and 1960s repositioned themselves in light of the analytical schema I've introduced for understanding what is at stake in the so-called return of ethnicity and the reconfiguration of cultural difference, which I believe has become a critical feature of our post-Enlightenment, late modern moment of globalization. With reference to the British context, let me therefore narrate what I see as the key discursive shifts entailed in what I am calling the ambiguous "return of ethnicity" under the conditions of globalization.

Following the end of the assimilationist dream and the positive revalorization of the discourse of difference, a debate ensued from the 1970s onward among the movements against racial discrimination and oppression in the United Kingdom. Multiculturalism became a dirty word. It was taken to signify those patronizing occasions of cultural pluralism, so symptomatic of the earlier moment (and familiar to those of us who were already in the United Kingdom as students when the wave of working-class black migration began), when we would be invited by some well-meaning and enlightened white church or community group to prepare our "ethnic food," wear our "ethnic dress," and perform songs in our "ethnic languages." I searched my wardrobe without success for even a hint of an ethnic costume so as to participate in the "spectacle of ethnicity," as I called it. Multiculturalism came to be seen as a willful diversion from, a deliberate occlusion of, the deeper structures of institutionalized racial disadvantage operative in housing, education, employment, wages, working conditions, and welfare. It was seen as hiding the nastier forms of racial prejudice and racism that had become part of the daily life of ordinary working black migrant families. Multiculturalism, it was argued, addressed only racism's surface effects, and matters were compounded by the traditional left orthodoxy, which held that, in any event, class and material issues were primary, and cultural issues were secondary and superstructural.

Antiracism thus emerged in the 1970s as the binary opposite of multiculturalism and became a signifier of a radically left set of campaigning political strategies. Significantly, this was the moment when, privileging race over cultural difference, the signifier "black" became the organizing and mobilizing category of identification that was adopted by both Afro-Caribbeans and Asians, so it included Sikh, Hindu, Muslim, Bangladeshi and other cultural groups from the Indian subcontinent, as well as Jamaicans, Trinidadians, Barbadians, and other "small islanders" from the Caribbean. As a result, "black" was made visible in its functioning as a discursive-political identity, a badge of identification adopted by different cultural groups in their struggle against racism, in place of an ethnic signifier referring to the content of distinct cultural characteristics.

This practice of calling yourself black was never universal. On the one hand, there were some migrants, from the Indian subcontinent especially, perhaps less involved in active antiracist politics, who felt they could not as easily identify with a term for a racialized cultural identity that more obviously referenced Afro-Caribbean people, for whom black signified those "grosser physical differences of color, hair and bone" that we have already examined. But on the other hand, the identification of Afro-Caribbean youth in the 1970s—through the adoption of the insignia and languages of Rastafarianism and the metaphorical identification it constructed between them and the symbolic homelands of the Caribbean and Africa—deepened the cultural content of, and gave cultural specificity to, the signifier "black." As the tide of the radical antiracism associated with the

1970s and the period following the urban rebellions of 1981 has ebbed during the 1980s and 1990s, cultural questions have climbed the agenda. As cultural politics has increasingly become the cutting edge of the struggles around racial oppression and marginalization, we have seen the relative decline, though not the disappearance, of the signifier "black," which made common cause of political alliances between Asians and Afro-Caribbeans. Nevertheless, the fragmentation of the scene into a proliferation of various ethnic identities that rank their cultural specificity seems to herald the coming of an American version of pluralist multiculturalism, as today in the United Kingdom not only is cultural difference increasingly emphasized, but the specificity of different cultural traditions has also become central to the construction of identities, each conceived in very particularistic, homogeneous, culturally self-enclosed, and self-sufficient ways. A form of ethnic identity politics has thus gradually gained ascendency over . . . well, over what? I was tempted to say these developments in the 1990s have gained ascendency over the politics produced around the racial signifier "black." But, as I have suggested, this was not, in the U.K. context, *racial* in any of the obvious and accepted senses of the term, since it was a signifier that won identification from, and thus succeeded in mobilizing, different groups—Asians and Afro-Caribbeans—who could hardly be said to belong to the same race, and who shared very few of the "grosser" physical or biological differences except one, color, and even that only in the loosest and most metaphorical sense in which one might refer to "people of color," in the United States, or to "nonwhites" more broadly.

"Black" was a political signifier because its narrative of identification suggested that the similarity that unified these groups who took it on as a "badge," as Du Bois would put it—who identified with it as a signifier of the experience of racial oppression and exclusion on the basis of color, and who expressed their political opposition to marginalization on the grounds of race—was greater than the difference that tended to divide them, whether morphology, language, history, custom, or religion. Despite the militant adoption of an antiracist banner, we can see how the politics of such movements actually functioned discursively: through the operation of the sliding signifier, and its relations of similarity and difference, as these developments took shape with the break from liberal humanist and universalist discourses.

The other dimension that tended to unite the two groups, Asians and Afro-Caribbeans, politically was the shared history of colonization and imperialism. One of the features that this aspect of my narrative foregrounds, in the contrast between antiracist politics in the United Kingdom during the 1970s and 1980s and the new global politics of cultural difference today, is the way in which the shared legacy of colonization and imperialism, or the contradictions between first world and third world, between the West and the rest, sometimes complements and reinforces what Du Bois called the shared social legacy of slavery, but at other times dislocates, interrupts, and stands in an overlapping yet disjunctive relationship with that legacy. In the new politics of cultural difference, this is one of those fault lines of historical specificity that both intersects the assumed unity of experience and identity among diaspora blacks and, on another dimension, fractures any assumed, given, or guaranteed political unity between blacks and other ethnic minority groups. What results is not the convergence of struggles but an all too familiar postmodern problem: the proliferation of social antagonisms. We may see the shift I have just described—the decline of "black" relative to the ascendency of more discrete ethnic identities in the United Kingdom since the 1980s—as one aspect of the larger phenomenon that is the "return to ethnicity." There are parallels, although not exactly the same, in the United States with the troubled relations between blacks and Chicanos and other Latinos, Koreans, Vietnamese, Chinese, and other nonwhite ethnic groups of the 1980s migration into America. What we have here, then, is an emergent field of racial, cultural, and ethnic difference and contestation in the late twentieth century that is articulated in different ways in different places. I would define this as a proliferating and fragmenting field of antagonism and cultural contestation that refuses to become a unified and sutured space of political representation, instead remaining a field of difference articulated in its relatively dislocated and disaggregated form as a site of generalized antagonism.

To complicate the picture even more, what I am calling the "return to ethnicity," which privileges cultural difference over the politics of antiracism, is not the end of the story. In the United Kingdom, the ascendancy of discrete ethnic identities already occupies the same discursive terrain as another, rival signifier: "black British," with the second word of the phrase now being given a problematic inflection by the first. This term, too, takes the national culture as the site of contestation, but it tends to cut across rather than reinforce racialized and ethnic boundaries between Afro-Caribbeans and Asians. This signifier is rapidly gaining ground today, especially among the third generation of both groups in the United Kingdom. If you like puzzling over taxonomies and what they tell us about how identities are constructed and mobilized through the shifting of signifiers in political struggle, then you might like to reflect on the similarities and differences within and across the diasporas of the "black Atlantic," Paul Gilroy's generative concept. In light of this, it is striking to note that black Americans moved to adopt the dignified, often hyphenated, ethnicized national designation "African American" in the very same moment—a moment of the ethnicization of racial taxonomies—as black Caribbean and Asian migrant communities in the United Kingdom began, hesitantly, to assent to the racialized national identity "black British," which you could say is also a moment of the ethnicization of the nation.

I hope I have said enough to support the claim that, in the discourses of cultural difference that have assumed much greater significance in our post-Enlightenment world, "ethnicity" is every bit as much a discursive construct, a sliding signifier, as "race." Indeed, in the taxonomies of cultural difference, and in the play of identities and identifications that is the serious stroke behind this discursive game, ethnicity and race continue to play hide-and-seek with one another. The idea with which we started, that the discourses of cultural difference would be able to resolve the problems engendered by the discursive operations of race, was overly optimistic, as it turns out.

Late Modern Globalization

So why, then, are we witnessing the return of ethnicity, the positive reevaluation of *ethnos,* not only in the examples I have given but as a worldwide phenomenon? How are we to understand and narrate what is happening globally around questions of cultural identity, cultural difference, and the politics of cultural representation in these postcolonial, post-Enlightenment times, which also seem to be postnational—that is, when the Western imperial nation-state may be a thing of the past. I emphasize the conjunctural moment because its transitional and unsettled character is really what the prefix *post-*registers for me, underlining the question of what we are coming after, what we are in the wake of, without being in any achieved sense beyond its reverberating effects, and without being able to name any new condition toward which we are definitively headed. Indeed, this ubiquitous prefix carries more than a hint that the transition may be a permanent state of affairs—transition without termination, dislocated times without the promise of supersession.

Thus *postcolonial* means after the epoch when imperial power was exercised by direct colonization, but it also means an era when everything still takes place in the slipstream of colonialism and hence bears the inscription of the disturbances that colonization set in motion. The term indicates a moment when everything in the conversation makes reference to the colonizing dominant, to the West, which may be resisted, but whose presence as an active force, as an interlocutor, cannot be denied, since the configurations that characterized the earlier epoch remain visible and operative, having real effects. So one might say postcolonial in the same sense that *poststructuralism* is the theoretical moment after a not completely superseded structuralism, which is still being referred to in the theoretical positions that poststructuralism is trying to displace. It follows too, then, that *postmodernism* is the time after modernism, a time that is unthinkable except as a reversal and a rearticulation of the discourse of modernism, which gives us modernism in the streets, not just in the gallery. And *deconstruction* is the time after the grand narratives of Western metaphysics and modernity, but a time that is unable to transcend the discursive limit points against which its own antifoundationalism is directed. Under such circumstances, cultural identities would be another concept now placed "under erasure," for precisely the embodied forms of cultural identity and difference that were constituted by the great discourses of modernity—imperial, national, racial, ethnic, masculine, ethnocentric, heterosexual—are now simultaneously decentered *and* reconfigured in new combinations. So how, in our global times, is cultural identity to be constituted and narrated?

What is powerfully dislocating cultural identities at the end of the twentieth century is a complex of processes and forces of change that, for convenience, can be summed up under the term "globalization." By globalization we mean the comprehensive integration of economic production, markets, financial systems, information flows, and technologies across the globe, alongside the worldwide movement of capital, goods, media messages and images, and people, with the disruption of settled borders, real and symbolic, as a result. Globalization refers to these intersecting processes, which increasingly cut across national frontiers, integrating and connecting nation-states, national cultures, diverse communities, and organizations into new space-time combinations that make the world, in reality and in experience, more interconnected. All of this implies the decline of the classical political idea of the sovereign nation-state, the classical economic concept of the self-regulating national economy, and the classical sociological conception of society as a sutured totality; the last of these now being displaced by a perspective that looks at how social life is ordered through overlapping and discontinuous times and spaces.[11]

Such space-time compressions, or disjunctures of distances and temporalities, are among the most significant features of globalization with a direct bearing on questions of identity and culture. Time and space are, after all, the basic coordinates of all systems of representation, as David Harvey has incisively demonstrated in *The Condition of Postmodernity*.[12] Every medium of representation—writing, drawing, painting, photography, telecommunications, information systems—must translate its subject into spatial and temporal dimensions. Thus literary narratives translate events into beginning-middle-end time sequences, and visual systems of representation translate three-dimensional objects into two dimensions. In his exciting book *The Black Atlantic,* Paul Gilroy speaks of trying to change how we represent the story of black music from a linear one, where African authenticity gives way to American inauthenticity, to a "two-way traffic between African cultural forms and the political cultures of the diasporas." He introduces the idea of a shift "from the chronotope of the road to the chronotope of the crossroads,"[13] borrowing Bakhtin's notion of the chronotope as "a unit of analysis for studying texts according to the ratio and nature of temporal and spatial categories represented ... an optic for reading texts as x-rays of the forces at work in the culture system from which they spring."[14] Homi Bhabha, looking at similar questions but now in a postcolonial frame rather than a postslavery context, defines the relations between the colonizer and the colonized in terms of disjunctive temporalities in which "the colonial" can only repeat itself in "the colonized" at a distance, with a destabilizing difference, through a series of dissimulating figures, with mimicry, parody, and grotesque realism being only some of the many loops through which the colonized occupy the interstice or gap "in between" these disjunctive temporalities so as to turn back and radically unsettle the linear time of Enlightenment modernity.[15] Questions of memory and radical disjunctures among time signatures in Toni Morrison's *Beloved* function in the same way to renarrate the experience of slavery in the African American context.[16]

The shaping and reshaping of space-time relationships within different discursive systems of representation have profound effects for how identities are narrated and understood. All identities are located in symbolic space and time. Like sexuality, they take place in the "field of vision," as Jacqueline Rose suggests in her book of that name, and vision always has its spatial coordinates, real or imaginary, in a field or the overall gestalt in which the subject is perceptually "placed." One might say that the mirror stage, which for Jacques Lacan is the very site of imaginary identification, is precisely such a theater of spatial-speaking relations regarding such placement among the different parts of the self, and between the self and its reflection in the gaze of the other.[17] To say that all identities are located or imagined in symbolic space and time is thus to say that we can see cultural identities as "landscaped," as having an imagined place or symbolic "home," a *heimat*. In addition to their placings in time—in narratives of the self, in our own life stories, in invented traditions binding past and present into myths of origin that project the current moment to the archaic past, and in narratives of the nation that connect the individual to larger events on a collective scale—we need to grasp the full significance for cultural identity of the spatial relations that Edward Said called "imaginary geographies."[18]

Place is one of those strong representational coordinates of cultural identity. It matters both as a dense, particular, local site where many relationships have overlapped across time, producing a richly textured sense of the ways in which space is grounded by distinctive ways of life, and as a kind of symbolic guarantee of stable, continuous, cultural patterns consistently reproduced through traditions that mirror the stability of kinship and blood ties among a settled, gathered, and interrelated population. These particular coordinates of space and time are especially important for what I would call the "strong" version of cultural identity inscribed by the concept of ethnicity, where social activities, common worlds, and all-encompassing systems of meaning are imagined as taking place in the same real or highly specific landscape, a place fixed discursively at another level by shared blood ties of family and kinship, and thus to a certain degree, perhaps, by shared physical features or characteristics. Where a people share not only a language or common customs but an *ethnos,* their sense of being bound to or belonging to the group is especially strong, and their version of cultural identity thereby becomes markedly confined and homogeneous as a result. Indeed, ethnicity in this strong sense is a form of cultural identity that, though in fact historically and culturally constructed, is powerfully tied to a sense of place and of group origins that comes to be so unified on many levels over a long period—across generations, across shared social space, and across shared histories—that it is experienced and imagined by many not as a discursive construction but as having acquired the durability of nature itself. Although discursively constructed, the strong sense of the *ethnos* of a community as having been transmitted through natural inheritance, as imprinted and inherited outside what we would call the play of history and culture, as if through the natural laws of descent, points to this version of ethnicity as the discursive form in which cultural identity appears as part of "kith and kin," rooted in "blood and soil." Ethnicity in this strong sense helps us to imagine culture as being simultaneously "at home" and as "home" itself, the place where we originally came from, which first stamped us with our original identity, from which there is no escape, and to which we are bonded by ties that are inherited and obligatory, the separation from which is painfully repeated in every other subsequent loss that we experience.

You may recall that in my first lecture I described the discursive work that race as a sliding signifier performs in constituting a chain of equivalences that enables us to read off from the visible signs of "the grosser physical differences of color, hair and bone" those meanings that come to be fixed back down the chain, as it were, in the biological and the genetic, and that are fixed further up the chain, as referring to the cultural and the civilizational. I now want to suggest that ethnicity not only functions within the same discursive chain as race but also operates in similar ways, that is to say, as a sliding signifier. Thus, whereas race is grounded in the biological and slides toward the cultural, *ethnos* or ethnicity in the strong sense that I've just described appears to be grounded exclusively in the cultural, in the realm of shared languages, specific customs, traditions, and beliefs, *yet it constantly slides*—especially through commonsense conceptions of kinship—toward a transcultural and even transcendental fix in common blood, inheritance, and ancestry, all of which gives ethnicity an originary foundation in nature that puts it beyond the reach of history.

My argument here is that, in addition to its many other dislocating effects, globalization powerfully fractures the temporal and spatial coordination of the systems of representation for cultural identity and imagined community that are at stake in the concept of "ethnicity," with the decisive result that identity is nowadays increasingly *homeless,* so to speak. Anthony Giddens speaks of the separation of space from place that is effected by globalization in its late modern forms. Whereas place is imagined as specific, concrete, known, and familiar—as the site of social practices that have formed and shaped our lives over long periods of time—what Giddens argues, with regard to space, is that

> in pre-modern societies, space and place largely coincided, since the spatial dimensions of social life are, for most of the population, dominated by "presence"—by localized activities. The advent of modernity increasingly tears space away from place by fostering relations between "absent" others, locationally distant from any given situation of face-to-face

interaction. In conditions of modernity... locales are thoroughly penetrated by and shaped in terms of social influences quite distant from them.[19]

It follows from this that one of the consequences of the recent forms and intensification of late modern globalization is to force us to abandon, as Doreen Massey argues, "the notion of places simply as settled, enclosed, and internally coherent," and to seek instead "its replacement or supplementation by a concept of place as meeting-place, the location of the intersection of particular bundles of activity spaces, of connections and interrelations, of influences and movements."[20] Such thinking underpins the view that place "is the vast complexity of the interlocking and articulating nets of social relations... always formed by particular sets of social relations and by the effects which juxtaposing those interrelations produce."[21]

Despite such developments, however, globalization is not a recent phenomenon per se. We could say it was inaugurated in the moment at the end of the fifteenth century when Europe, having expelled its others—Jews and Muslims—turned outward and the Euro-imperial adventure we call modernity began on a global scale.

The dislocation of a world composed of settled, kin-bound, territorially unified peoples began, then, with exploration and conquest, colonization and slavery, as I have discussed elsewhere.[22] The first tentative formation of a capitalist and commodity-based market economy took the form of a global rather than regional or continental phenomenon. Where Karl Marx famously stated, apropos the dislocating effects of this world system, "all that is solid melts into the air," one might add that in its late modern incarnation, globalization has simply acquired a new intensification of this effect, which has assumed new forms.[23] But even though capitalism and the world market long ago intersected the homogeneous cultural spaces that underpinned traditional conceptions of collective identity, it is striking to note that such versions of "imagined community," in Benedict Anderson's sense, have largely remained intact until recently, since the nostalgia for community, for shared culture, is one of modernity's consistently compensatory and consoling refrains.[24] There is now considerable evidence that late modern globalization as we are experiencing it is further undermining and putting into crisis those centered and unified formations of cultural identity, including that most powerful of modern identities, the nation. Such evidence of a loosening of identification with the national culture suggests that what we are witnessing is a strengthening of cultural flows and collective ties that operate "above" and "below" the level of the nation-state, functioning on interpenetrating scales that disrupt our conventional distinctions of locality, neighborhood, and region.

Some cultural theorists of late modernity argue that there is now an overwhelmingly powerful trend toward global interdependence that is leading to the breakdown of all strong identities. The dissolution of our older idea—or was it a fantasy?—of "the local" produces a fragmentation of cultural codes, a multiplicity of styles mediated by current technology, an emphasis on the ephemeral, and a celebration of difference within contemporary cultural pluralism, all of which passes under the name of the *global postmodern.*[25] Cultural flows within globalized consumerism, however uneven they may be and however far they are dominated by the West, have been said to create the possibility of new kinds of transnationally shared identities, even if the process of sharing among people widely separated in space, time, and cultural conditions is mediated by the status of the participants as customers for more of the same goods, as clients for more of the same services, and as audiences for more of the same images.[26] People in remote villages in poor third-world countries can today receive in the privacy of their homes the messages and images of the rich consumer cultures of the West, which are the privileged content transmitted by global television or the ubiquitous radio, satellite, and other information systems that bind those on the former periphery into the new global networks. Jeans and sneakers, the uniform of the young in Western popular culture, are as omnipresent in Southeast Asia as in the United States or the United Kingdom, not only because they are often actually manufactured in Taiwan, Hong Kong, or South Korea for shops in London, New York, Los Angeles, Paris, or Rome, but also because of the growth of the worldwide marketing of the Western youth consumer image culture as well. It is hard, under such conditions, to think of Indian cooking as something expressive of the authentic "ethnic" traditions of the South Asian subcontinent when there are at least two Indian restaurants on the main streets of every town and city in Britain. In London's East End, Tower Hamlets, or the Isle of Dogs, for instance, "going for a curry" is the favorite way for National

Front skinheads to warm up before an evening's entertainment of beating up Bangladeshi youths; the combination is now as "English" as a cup of tea.

Yet for all of these examples of the global postmodern, cultural homogenization is the fast-growing orthodox narrative of globalization as a transnational strategy. Since there is a distinct power geometry to it—it being easier to "eat ethnic" in Los Angeles than it is in Calcutta—this is a narrative that I observe to be particularly seductive for critical intellectuals in the West. There is, no doubt, a great deal of truth in it. All the same, it is in my view a one-sided account of cultural exploitation—a tale with which to frighten little children. Let me try to say, quietly, what I believe is wrong with this way of conceptualizing the effects of globalization, and what is wrong, by extension, with the equally homogenizing and essentializing conception of "ethnicity," which, by its absent presence in the discourse of lament, underpins the narrative of cultural homogeneity as its mirror opposite.

One objects to this thesis, first, because the most striking aspect of the newer forms of globalization is the appearance, alongside the tendencies toward homogenization, of the *proliferation of difference* of all sorts. Only some of these developments are effectively harnessed to the global market, which in any event moves and responds as much by exploiting diasporas as by regulating them; it uses forms of niche marketing in which tapping into marginal advantages produces fluctuating effects of which capital is only in partial control. What the cultural homogenization narrative loses sight of is that the march of global capital is accompanied by the unexpected revival and return of new kinds of local identifications, new forms of symbolic attachments to the connotations of place and cultural specificity, and new discursive formations of the traditional. Even in matters of taste and style that span the vast distances integrated by the new global technologies and which link together the various times and spaces of capital turnover in production, there has emerged a new symbolic "tribalism," as Alberto Melucci calls it, alongside the consumer homogenization story of Coca-Cola, Big Macs, Nike sneakers, and CNN broadcasts everywhere.[27] What else is street style or "street cred," or the symbolic global significance of place names such as Bed-Stuy, Brixton, or Trenchtown as they circulate in the new world musics of rap and reggae, if not a marking of locality, with its connotations of place, as a response to the forces of homogenization? We see other such cases of an emphasis on the local in forms of popular culture in Japan and Southeast Asia.

There is a difference, of course, between the forms of difference that are harnessed to and permeated by the capitalist market and other forms of marking cultural difference that represent fissures, breaks, or fault lines in the cultural system that the market has to negotiate. The fact that there is negotiation means we are not dealing with absolute difference. But where would you draw the line in rap or reggae between differences permeated by the market and differences that signify social ruptures? Certainly these new localisms that emerge with the proliferation of difference are not simply a repetition of the primordial and homogenizing attachments that place names may have been taken to signify in the past; instead they function, as Kevin Robbins argues, as a new kind of "local" that acquires specific meaning by operating within a larger, globalized cultural *topos*.[28] Such localisms as "Bed-Stuy" indicate the movement of a reconfiguration of ethnicity, marking looser, more porous, more open-ended, and increasingly hybridized forms of cultural identity, which are thus the site not of the unilateralist triumph of the global postmodern but of something more difficult, complex, and historically specific, namely, new articulations between "the local" and "the global" that cannot be mapped within the terms of nations and national cultures as we might have tried to do in the past. The proliferation of such cultural differentiations confronts us with articulations of differences and similarities that no longer cohere within a single cultural, discursive, or political framework; these new forms of articulation of the local and the global cannot be convened, as it were, under the roof of a single identity, all overlapping in the same space. The prolific spread of such cultural differentiations produces something more diverse, more fragmented, more discontinuous, and less sutured than anything that has come before, giving rise to often contradictory articulations across spaces, times, and discourses that produce complex points of cultural identification—positionalities that tend to dislocate rather than reprise one another. Nevertheless, such developments and tendencies are critical for our story since this is how "difference" is more and more actually being produced and negotiated in our world. It is precisely from such hybridized and incomplete foci of difference that many new identifications are arising. The production of new points of identification—as well as the return to and revival of old ones, which I shall come back to in a moment—

is thus an all-important key to the emergence of what we may call the reconfiguration of ethnicity under the conditions of the global postmodern.

A second objection to the cultural homogenization narrative stems from the way this story, with its built-in oscillation between the binary poles of "tradition" and "modernity," not to speak of Antonio Gramsci's old friends "pessimism of the intellect" and "optimism of the will," recapitulates and repeats the assumptions of the Enlightenment grand narrative. Liberalism and Marxism, which were both in their different ways Enlightenment grand narratives in that they sought to tell stories of human progress, led us to expect that those old ties and bonds of symbolic attachment to place, tribe, locality, religion, and landscape would be gradually but remorselessly swept aside by the advance of capitalist modernity, commodifying, rationalizing, and thereby homogenizing everything in its wake. Marxism's logic of capital and liberalism's drive toward secularization and universalism are, in this sense at least, not antithetical but mirror discourses of each other.

But in my view, the ways that liberalism and Marxism alike tell the story of modernity are one-sided and incomplete. Capitalist modernity has always advanced as much by way of the production and negotiation of difference as it has through enforcing sameness, standardization, and homogenization. Those who know capitalist modernity at the periphery always know that in Latin America and Africa, with their dependent economies of the interior and their neocolonial or export sectors integrated into the world market unevenly, it is the exploitation of difference—the taking advantage of differentials, and not the standardization of economic variables—that pushes the story of capitalist modernity remorselessly onward. This applies equally to the combination of tribal homelands, migrant labor camps, and segregated residence in South Africa until recently, and was indeed an underpinning to New World slavery itself in the Americas and the Caribbean, where unfree and forced labor exist in a differential relationship that is foundational to the so-called free market of the global capitalist economy. What we see at both the periphery and the center of the system is that differences have been gendered, sexualized, and classed as well as being ethnicized and racialized as a condition of the functioning of the world market.

One sometimes suspects that in the face of such complexities of articulation, in both past and present configurations of Western modernity, there is a degree of collusion among the various identities connected by trade and so on. It is true that globalization, whether early modern or late modern, is a combined and uneven process, with dramatically differential effects in different places and in different strata. Both the corporate executive in his business-class seat aboard a jumbo jet flying from Jeddah to Tokyo and the Arab desert traveler on his camel moving between oases over which the former unwittingly passes are postmodern "nomads" in the sense that each occupies very distinct time-space trajectories. Nevertheless, the fact is that ever since the onset of the Euro-imperial adventure, global times and spaces have never peacefully coexisted but have been brutally truncated and condensed into one overarching, dominant, abstract, and imperial chronotope, which is the time of the West. The societies of the periphery have never been the closed hinterlands they have been represented to be, for they have always been open to Western cultural influences and vice versa. The idea that the colonial peripheries are closed spaces, ethnically pure, culturally traditional, and forever undisturbed in what Claude Lévi-Strauss called the "old zones of history until yesterday" is merely a fantasy about otherness, a colonial fantasy maintained about the periphery by the West, which tends to like its natives pure, its beaches empty, and its exotic places to be faraway and untouched by human hands.[29]

Another consequential effect of staging the process of globalization in terms of a static opposition between two essentialized objects of discourse—their "backwardness" and our globally modern "advancement"—is the way in which such an approach tends to construe the symbolic reconfiguration of ethnicity today as necessarily a form of fundamentalism, a refusal of modernity, which makes it, by definition, regressive, archaic, and atavistic. I will come back to this way of thinking about the return to ethnicity when I discuss the category of "nation" in my third lecture. Nevertheless, to the extent that such a binary between "backward" and "advanced" is embedded in commonsense discourses of tradition and modernity, one would hardly believe that the new forms of cultural identity and identification arising with the current forms of globalization have also been profoundly important sites of resistance.

This last point brings me to a third objection to the globalization-as-homogenization narrative: that this narrative not only is unable to countenance a politics of resistance but also cannot account for the production of new identities as they arise under late modern conditions. One has only to think of the role played in national liberation and decolonization struggles by the idea of a people and a culture that predate colonialism (however much it functioned as a foundational myth, a necessary fiction), or the role that the symbolic recall of "Africa" played in the renarrativization of history that led in the 1960s and 1970s to the civil rights movement in the United States and the cultural revolution that transformed the British West Indies into a "black" space for the first time since slavery, to realize that what twentieth-century history confronts us with is the *production of new subjects* and not the mere repetition of old ones. As a way of understanding that what is at issue in the return of ethnicity today is the production of identities and identifications, rather than the uncovering of essences given in nature, one might equally recall how an idea of "Africa"—not a place actually located on any map but a country of the mind—alone enabled young children of Caribbean migrants, the second generation, to survive life in the United Kingdom in the 1970s. It was cultural forms such as the music technology of the recording studio, the sound system, and the vinyl disc, as much as the metaphorical languages of Rastafarianism, that allowed them not just to survive but also to acquire the sense of self-pride, the symbolic centeredness, and their own way of styling their bodies that characterized their new ways of being—or rather "becoming"—black in the postwar history of multicultural Britain.

The view that any of these highly complex and variable forms of new ethnicity, whether in African America, black Britain, or the Caribbean, could be understood, deciphered, or explained away as simply a return to "backwardness" is simply laughable. One could much more easily and convincingly make the case that what one sees in such phenomena is precisely the doubling—the Janus face—of ethnicity in global times, which compels our attention toward the discursive effects of doubleness, reversal, and transcoding that are its characteristic symbolic and cultural features. Above all, what such new ethnicities confront us with is the symbolic "detour" to the present that moves through the past, marking the site of collective investment in stakes made on the future within these difficult, more vernacular experiences of modernity. How else could one begin to make sense of the fact that the varieties of black cultural identity present in Britain today, whose genealogy I traced at the start of this lecture, are simultaneously the site of continuing marginalization and exclusion, being the objects of material and symbolic practices of racialized oppression, *and also* the signifiers of a new kind of ethnicized modernity, close to the cutting edge of a new iconography and a new semiotics that are redefining "the modern" itself?

I still have something to say in the final lecture about those equally late modern forms of the reconfiguration of ethnicity that do indeed present themselves as a recovery of lost origins, as a reproduction of originary culture, as a mere repetition of the same, all of which concern ethnicity as a form of cultural absolutism or fundamentalism. But I want to hold on to the contradictory tension by which, through a particular and distinctive form of marking cultural difference, historically marginalized and oppressed peoples also exploit the global proliferation of difference *to produce themselves as new subjects,* emerging through a symbolic detour that critically reprises the discursively constructed past, and who thereby enter our contemporary moment through a certain kind of reethnicization of the cultural politics of difference.

3

NATIONS AND DIASPORAS

IN MY SECOND lecture I spoke of the contradictory ground that, under the impact of globalization, world migration, and the consequent uneven multiculturalization of daily life, is emerging as the contemporary terrain of cultural conflict—this is the "return of ethnicity" as a sliding and ambivalent signifier in the cultural politics of difference that characterizes our late modern, global moment. Against the grain, I spoke of some of the positive forms and effects that have followed the decisive break with Enlightenment universalism, and hence I stressed the subsequent revalorization of difference among social movements. However, rather than simply recognizing the transvaluation of the signifiers of difference, or translating the signifier "ethnicity" from the negative to the positive pole, let me now try to unsettle the term a little bit more so as to bring out some of its contradictory features, and thus to deconstruct what is, for some, its disarming seductiveness. I want to do this by introducing my third term, the discourse of "nation," which has a complex and ambivalent relationship to both race and ethnicity that I will briefly and selectively trace. To go back to my previous argument: the reason "culture" and "cultural difference" cannot be unproblematically substituted for "race" and "racial difference" as a way of holding in check the biologized signifier, which continues to secure the various meanings and discourses of race in place, is because the signifier of cultural difference—"ethnicity"—is itself Janus-faced, contradictory, sutured, and stitched up, and as such is always in danger of sliding culture toward nature.

But first I need to be clear why this question of cultural difference matters, and to say something about the nature of the discursive shift that I believe to have taken place in the latest phase of globalization. Cultural difference matters because, in my sights, everyone has an ethnicity in the loosest sense of the term. It is as integral to identity as our sexuality or our nationality. That is to say, the signifiers of cultural difference—language, history, values, beliefs, customs, rituals, traditions, and worlds of meaning—are all key elements in the discourses in which identification is constituted, transformed, and

contested. I speak here of the process of *identification*—
of taking up positions of identity—rather than identity as a fixed essence, because identification in this
sense is never complete, is always in process; yet for
this very reason, such processes of identification are
constantly caught in, and re-formed through, the
shifting of the markers of difference, as well as our
changing subjective investment in the positionalities
into which we are interpellated. In this sense, then,
identity is precisely *not* fixed by the simple repetition
through time of an originary essence or by the teleological unfolding of some inner "real me" toward an
end that is somehow identical to itself or known in
advance.

Identity cannot be a fixed essence at all, as if it lay
unchanged outside of history and culture, and this
is so for one principal reason: identity is not given
once and for all by something transmitted in the
genes we carry in the color of our skin, but is shaped
and transformed historically and culturally. This is
the discursive dimension of identity that I keep re-
turning to throughout these lectures. Identity is not
a fixed origin to which we are attached by the harness
of tradition, an origin to which we can make some
final and absolute return. On the other hand, it
does not follow that we should replace the Cartesian

conception of the subject with the free-floating "nomadic" subject put forward in some of the post-modern alternatives.[1] Cultural identity is always specific, grounded through the marking of similarity and difference, and this is my crucial emphasis, for it is such a process of discursive marking that gives every cultural identity its histories and its languages. Moreover, these conditions of identification always have real, material, and symbolic effects.

Without its specific histories, identity would not have the symbolic resources with which to construct itself anew. Without its various languages, identity would be deprived of the capacity to enunciate—to speak and to act in the world. To locate oneself within a language is to take up its interdiscursive field of meanings. And since all identities must significantly mark their similarity to and difference from something else—for meaning is always relational and positional—then every identity, however provisionally it asserts itself, must always have a symbolic "other," which is what defines its constitutive outside. The difference lies not in whether there is, in fact, such an other to which our identities relate, but in whether the representation of that difference, that relationship to others, is fixed and degraded, so it becomes the object of symbolic violence, as in the operations of power in Hegel's master/slave dialectic, for instance, or whether the discursive inscription of difference is able to establish with others a dialogic relationship to alterity that, within this more Bakhtinian and Levinasian framework, can never be fixed and finalized but is always ongoing and in process.[2]

To think of the historical conditions that shape identity in this way is to say that the past continues to speak to, in, and through us, although it has many voices and therefore always has the discursive character of what Bakhtin calls the "multiaccentual," as all meaning does since it defines the very ground of culture. Without the past we would not be able to enunciate, because to enunciate is to position oneself within language and thereby to assume the fiction that one possesses a finished identity. But this past, while formative—giving each enunciation, each positional identity, its historical and cultural specificity—cannot address or shape us as a simple, originary, factual past that *guarantees* that our identity will remain the same and ever identical to itself. Instead of it being a matter of guarantees, one might say that our relationship to the past, as it marks the positions from which we speak, is analogous to the child's relationship to the mother: what the subject relates to is the imaginary conception of the origin as a plenitude, that is to say a past whose illusory fullness and completedness is always postulated, in Lacanian terms, "after the break"—*within* the terms of culture, *within* the language of the symbolic. This is why, thereafter, our relation to the origin is always something that has to be *told*; it is why "the past" becomes available to us only insofar as it is something *narrated,* and it is also why such narration is itself always constructed partly through memory, desire, fantasy, and myth. Cultural identities are thus fixed not by any actual "return to the origin" but by the points of identification or suturing made within the discourses of history and culture, for the positioning of the subject in relation to its sense of the past is always a discursive matter. As I put it in another essay, identity is not a matter of essence but of positioning, and hence there is always a politics of identity, a politics of position and positionality that follows "the end of the innocent notion of the essential black subject," which can have no guarantee in an unproblematic, transcendental law of origin.[3] Hence I am arguing that cultural identities matter not because they fix us into place politically but because *they are what is at stake*—what is won or lost—in cultural politics.

As to the shift I tentatively tried to sketch in the second lecture with regard to the concept of ethnicity, one could reiterate the point by saying that what is in question, simply put, is a shift from identity to identification, from an understanding of identity as something defined by given attributes to a discursive conception of the subject as it is positioned by, and repositions itself within, various ensembles of discourse. Previously, "difference" was the effect of the Western discourses of otherness, the outcome of a dialectics of othering under colonial histories, of which, after Frantz Fanon, Edward Said, Sander Gilman, Gayatri Spivak, Homi Bhabha, and the postcolonial critics, we have come to learn so much.[4] The effect of the different forms of othering was to construct the many kinds of difference that are complexly distributed among the peoples of the globe within a binary order of representation so as to reduce, condense, and polarize such differences discursively. What resulted was a reductively simplistic and unpassable symbolic frontier, which thereby essentialized all the forms of difference into an us-versus-them opposition that operated through the dialectics of otherness. What we, in turn, inherited from such a system of representation was the notion of "civilization" against the "barbarians, which meant a negative or reactive identification for all those excluded by this operation. But what the reconfiguration of ethnicity signifies in the latter part of the twentieth century is that the difference so constituted has come to be transcoded, and actively embraced in the process, as a point of positive or affirmative identification among the oppressed and the excluded. Thus it now marks difference as the site of cultural contestation and cultural politics on a global scale.

It is crucial to understand the work of the discursive, since this is the form the terrain of the political assumes under global conditions today. What is at issue is not breaking with the system altogether and somehow going outside it to find its absolute opposite, but a shift that has been brought about by the transcoding, reversal, and rearticulation of the terms of the discursive system itself, thereby transforming the binaries of "the West versus the rest" into a weave of multiaccentual differences. This is a shift of historic dimensions, for it assumes the form of a struggle over the very making and remaking of *différance*. By spelling the term in the French way (which is not at all to be theoretically trendy but the reason I keep referring to Derrida), I underline the point that deconstruction is also, in philosophical terms, significantly located in the post-Enlightenment critique of the discourse of identity. Derrida's critique of what he calls "the metaphysics of presence" is a critique of any notion of an essence that is held to be identical to itself and fully present to itself. In these terms—and here I quote at length—*différance* means

> the movement according to which language, any code or system of referral in general, is constituted historically as a weave of differences. It is because of difference that the movement of signification is possible only if each so-called present element is related to something other than itself, thereby keeping within itself the mark of the past element, and already letting itself be articulated by the mark of the future element, this trace being related no less to what is called the future than to what is called the past . . . not in order to see opposition erase itself but to see what indicates that each of the terms must appear as the difference of the other, as the other different and deferred in the economy of the same.[5]

Translated into the politics of cultural difference, as it is grounded in the discourses of race and ethnicity, this account of the movement of signification is what, in my essay "Cultural Identity and Diaspora," I called the "play" of identity through difference, and it is a dynamic that Paul Gilroy, in his remarkable book on black diaspora experience, refers to as "the changing same."[6]

In a moment I'll suggest, however, that this is not the only form in which difference has reappeared and reasserted itself in global times. Indeed, in the current phase of globalization, we frequently find cultural difference, or what is sometimes called ethnicity, appearing *both* in its restricted, unified, closed, absolutist, defensive, and essentialist forms *and* as a "weave of differences" that is looser, more permeable, and more porous in character. The interplay between difference and *différance*—that is to say, the contradiction *inside* the very signification of difference rather than, as was the case previously, the fixed us-and-them polarization that opposed "their difference" (which meant nationalism) to "our identity" (which meant modernity)—is how the politics of cultural identity is now playing itself out on the global stage. Foregrounding nation within the discursive chain of race-ethnicity-nation is thus key for my demonstration of this double syntax at work in cultural politics today.

Whither Nation?

In the modern world, national cultures have been a powerful source of cultural and political identity.

"The idea of a man without a nation," Ernest Gellner once wrote, contrasting this with someone without a state, "seems to impose a far greater strain on the modern imagination. . . . A man must have a nationality as he must have a nose and two ears. [Women, I presume, need have neither. —S.H.] . . . All this seems obvious, though, alas, it is not true. But that it should have come to *seem* so very obviously true is indeed an aspect, perhaps the very core, of the problem of nationalism."[7] National cultures are, in this sense, distinctly modern in form, and Western nation-states have dominated the economic and political history of modernity. Yet I should also point out that in rehearsing a preliminary definition regarding nations we have already stumbled across something contradictory in the history of modernity. At one level, capitalism has, from its inception, worked through transnational flows of capital, trade, commodities, raw materials, and profits. But, to recall my argument in the second lecture—that capitalist modernity has worked as much through the proliferation of difference as it has through the homogenization of the world into sameness—I would stress that it is crucial to recognize that such flows have, until recently, been powerfully organized around, and thereby sustained within, the particularly boundaried formations of the nation-state, which gave rise to our commonplace notion of the "national economy" and the "national culture." As Immanuel Wallerstein observed of this paradox of capitalist modernity: "At the very moment one has been creating national cultures, each dislodges the other, and these flows (between and across national frontiers) have been breaking down national distinctions."[8]

Gellner himself certainly sees these national formations as engines of modernity. Not only did the national cultures of the modern Western nation-state help to create standards of universal literacy and generalize a single vernacular language throughout the nation, he argues, but they also broke the stranglehold of the church, thereby creating a homogeneous secular culture in the West, with the achievement of homogeneity being regarded as crucial to the maintenance of national cultural institutions. More significant is that the allegiances and identifications that in premodern times were given to tribe, people, religion, and region came gradually, in Western societies, to be transferred to the national culture. On this view, other differences may have persisted at the local level, but they were gradually subsumed beneath what Gellner calls the "political roof" of the nation-state. A powerful source of meaning for modern cultural identities thus emerges from the historical construction of the nation (although it has to be said that Gellner seems not to have heard of race, which is notably absent from his account).[9]

But, in fact, nations do not just emerge; they are formed. And national identities, moreover, are not attributes we are born with, but are formed and transformed within discourses and other systems of representation. We know what it is to be English, British, American, or Jamaican because of the ways that "Americanness" or "Britishness" or any of these other identities has come to be represented as a set of shared meanings within the national cultures in which they are shaped at different historical moments. Such discursive operations in the making of national cultural identities are always, of course, closely articulated to power and to the way power functions in society. We should think of the nation not only as a political entity but also as something that produces meaning and constructs identification. A nation is always a symbolic community, and it is this dimension which accounts for its "power to generate identity and allegiance," as Bill Schwarz has put it in his work on conservatism, nationalism, and imperialism.[10] It is precisely in this sense that the historian Benedict Anderson has argued that a national identity is an "imagined community," and in this sense too that, as the great British patriot and racist Enoch Powell put it, "the life of nations no less than that of men is lived largely in the imagination."[11]

Out of the many events of the past, the discourse of British nationalism, for instance, constructed a narrative of nation in which a set of legends, images, landscapes, and scenarios, as well as historical events, symbols, and rituals, all came to represent a unified story that served as a container for the shared experiences, griefs, sorrows, divisions, disasters, and triumphs of the people as they positioned themselves within, and came to be positioned by, such discourses of national belonging. It is this "story" that gives meaning to the nation as a world of meaning that constructs identification precisely because it helps us to see ourselves in the imaginary as somehow sharing in an overarching collective narrative, such that our humdrum, everyday existence comes to be connected with a great national destiny that existed prior to us and which will outlive us. The narrative of nation, in this sense, thus always projects "Englishness" or "Americanness" *out* of real time, *out* of the conflicts and discontinuities, *out* of the unevenness and differences that compose the actual state of the nation and the peoples of its history, and *into* a timeless register of mythic time. As Homi Bhabha has remarked, "Nations, like narratives, lose their origins in the myths of time and only fully realize their horizons in the mind's eye."[12] The focus on tradition and heritage constructs continuity as a key element in the stories that modern nations construct, smoothing out the discontinuities of a turbulent and contested history into the uninterrupted flow of a long, unbroken, organic evolution. Even if, as Eric Hobsbawm and Terence Ranger noted, these are invented traditions, "which appear or claim to be old but are often quite recent in origin,"[13] the emphasis on timeless continuity operates discursively to translate the confusions and setbacks of historical contingency into something that is to be made intelligible within some larger story, thereby snatching triumph from disaster, as we in the United Kingdom have seen in our stories of the Somme, Dunkirk, or the Falklands.

In fact, what is represented as originary, essential, and shared within national identity has always been constructed *across* difference and *through* difference because cultural distinctions of background and upbringing, of social class, of different ethnic and racial histories, of gender and sexuality, are the very stuff of which national identities are made. Questions of gender and sexuality are of particular importance, though I refer to them only marginally here, because—contrary to our received understanding—cultural identity has as its condition of existence not just discourses of race and ethnicity but also other dimensions of difference, and sexual difference in particular. Myths of Englishness, and indeed of Americanness, so far as I understand it, are powerfully stabilized by gender and sexuality. In the British case, national identity has been consistently constructed through the virtues said to be characteristic of certain kinds of men who become, for this very reason, the bearers of the national story. Constructed around "manly" virtues of self-discipline and self-restraint, stories of national valor and heroism in the narratives of Britishness are deeply caught up with the stiff-upper-lipped, understated, emotionally armor-plated, and buttoned-up values of certain kinds of English masculinity, which thus become representative of a certain generation and class. This gendering of national identity is, in turn, intimately related to the forging of the British nation as it is constitutively related to its imperial "others."

In her work on the role of the imperial in general, and on Jamaica in particular, within the English imaginary—and on the role of the enslaved and colonized other in the constitution of a specific version of white English masculinity in the nineteenth century, before the success of the liberal abolitionists in 1832 and the onset of a new kind of "separate species" racism in the 1860s—Catherine Hall has argued that white British identities, both masculine and feminine, had long been constituted in relation to imperial power and racialized others.[14] Not only, then, are national cultures, as systems of representation, and national identities, as ensembles of identification, constructed through and through by differences of various kinds, but the very idea of the nation is not as unambiguously modern as its liberal genealogy presupposes. The word *nation,* Timothy Brennan reminds us, refers "both to the modern nation-state and to something more ancient and nebulous—the *natio*—a local community, domicile, family, or condition of belonging."[15] Modern national identities represent the surreptitious attempts to bring together these two halves of the national equation—to complement the *political* unity of the nation-state with the underlying shared values and meanings of a national *culture*—or as Gellner disarmingly put it, "to make culture and polity congruent" and thereby endow "reasonably homogeneous cultures each with its own political roof."[16] This sought-for congruence between the political and the cultural was particularly important in the nineteenth century with regard to the right of peoples to national self-determination, but it was a major point of cultural difficulty and the site of much social and cultural engineering in plural migrant nations such as the United States, where the cultures to be covered by the political roof of the nation-state were palpably not homogeneous at all, or at least could not be made to seem so without a great deal of judicious stretching and no small degree of exclusion.

In fact, even the much more culturally homogeneous nation-states of western Europe consisted of disparate cultures whose various regional differences came to be unified only by the hegemony of one part of the national economy over the others, or by a lengthy process of violent conquest that entailed the forcible suppression and subordination of difference. The deep-seated ambivalence in the United Kingdom marks this fact, which we see in the sliding and shifting that goes on between the terms *English* and *British*. In relation to its constitutive imperial outside, the nation of the United Kingdom may be represented by the signifier "British," but in relation to the collective *natio*, as it is lived, everyone knows that Englishness prevails, as it is hegemonically sustained by its relations of power over the Scots, the Welsh, and the Irish. The British people are, by definition, the product of a series of such conquests and invasions, whether Celtic, Roman, Saxon, Viking, or Norman. Throughout Europe the story of conquest is repeated ad nauseam. What is more, most modern western European nation-states either were centers of empire or controlled neoimperial spheres of influence, exercising hegemony over the cultures of the colonized, and this too has come to trouble the stability and coherence that the narratives of the modern nation-state seek to secure.

We should think of national cultures, then, as discursive-like in their mode of constructing collective identity. Organized around the national signifier, whose function is to represent difference-as-unity, to make all of its constituent elements *present* as identity, modern nation-states have complex histories that are always crosscut by internal differences that come to be unified only by the exercise of cultural power. Making the political and the cultural fully congruent is something that can be achieved, if at all, only through an ongoing process of representation. Most of our modern nation-states are cultural hybrids—they are mongrelized and diasporized beyond repair, not that any self-respecting English-man would have, until recently, thought of himself as ethnic in any sense. Englishness is not an ethnicity in such a worldview: it is the norm against which, by angle of deviation, ethnicity is to be measured. Even the United States, which, as I argued earlier, has been obliged to understand itself as culturally and ethnically plural, always told itself the story, as Werner Sollors puts it, of "ethnicity plus one"—a formulation that acknowledges the constitutive outside that makes the significant marking of ethnic difference both possible and obligatory.[17]

In the nineteenth century, the term *race*—as in "the English race"—was consistently deployed as a commonplace way for popular and official discourses to refer to the distinctive rights, qualities, and destinies of the English as a people and as a culture: freeborn, tolerant, rational, individualist, wise, commonsensical, and touched by constitutional genius in the government of both their selves and their passions and interests, as David Hume called them. Here the discourse of Englishness reached through the terminology of race for what I have called the strong sense of ethnicity or cultural difference so as to evoke the *ethnos* of the British people. At issue is an idea so close to inheritance and descent through kinship, consanguinity, and blood—a world of meaning underpinned by the genealogies of class, family, and the long-term settlement of the land—that it functioned less as part of an actual history than as the making of a highly mythologized past, one in which history was completely naturalized. This was an image of the nation that worked discursively to secure difference so as to explain, above all, why the natural rights of freeborn Englishmen were *not* appropriate for emancipated slaves, or for women for that matter, or for Aborigines, or Hindus, or Hottentots, or Maoris, or Zulus. Another way to put this would be to say that even as the modern discourse of the nation sought to unify the United Kingdom's internal differences, the transformations of Englishness in the nineteenth century revealed that it became increasingly dependent on the imperial discourses of race.

In the latter third of the century, the era of scientific and ethnological racism, the racial signifier was regrounded in biological, morphological, and post-Darwinian evolutionary discourse, including eugenics. This development was European in scope and much propelled by the aftermath of, and reaction to, the abolition of slavery as well as by the intensification of the imperial adventure that climaxed in the so-called scramble for Africa following the carving up of the continent at the Berlin Congress of 1885. But, paradoxically, this hardening of the line of unbridgeable racialized difference between "us" and "them" coincided in Britain with the great suffusion, in popular culture and in the popular imaginary, of the sheer spectacle of empire. It was through this cultural operation that Benjamin Disraeli grounded a declining monarchy and its emblems in the hearts and affections of the British people, in the symbolic repertoire of the nation, and simultaneously in the iconography of the Conservative Party, thereby bringing off an unthinkable political conjuring trick—a popular and postdemocratic Toryism—and thereby unifying the nation as an imperial family across the divisions of class and gender.[18]

This imperialist conception of the British nation, stitched together and held in place by the representation of Englishness—and doubly underpinned by an essentializing reading of history and by evocations of the transhistorical "genius" or *ethnos* of the British people—was a story that survived until the postwar period. It was only in the 1950s and 1960s, when the loss of empire, economic decline, and the passing of the burden of world leadership to the United States were compounded by the great migrations from the

Caribbean and the Asian subcontinent, that this entire class-ethnic-gender-imperial-racial settlement began to disintegrate, precipitating what we can call a "crisis of identity" on the part of the British/English national culture. The fact that, after 1945, the empire had come home, Catherine Hall argues, led to a profound destabilizing of white identities in Britain, which raises what, until recently, was a literally unthinkable question: is it possible to be black and British?[19]

What is interesting here is that, in different ways and despite the specificities of the British case, we are witnessing a *similar and parallel phenomenon in all the Western nation-states as a consequence of globalization*. The crisis of identity among the post-Enlightenment, postimperial Western nation-states and their national cultures and national identities is today a global phenomenon of utmost significance. What is precipitating it, and what lies on its cutting edge, is not simply the internationalization of capital, with its modes of production and consumption, nor the weakening of the economic and political sovereignty of modern nation-states, which I referred to in my second lecture, but rather the joker in the pack, the element that really unfixes a certain conception of homogeneous national cultural identity and puts under erasure the whole notion of "one people, one *ethnos,* under one political roof," is mass migration.

Worldwide Migrations

It would be absurd for me to try to conjure up for you what you know only too well: the degree to which the always fragile and surprisingly sickly plant that we know as modern national identity has been thrown into crisis by the great planned and unplanned movements of peoples, roughly from the global South to the global North, in the wake of, and along the so-called track rails (or, better, the debt routes), of the current phase of globalization. But you may not have fully realized how much this is part of a larger global story that includes, first, the coming home of the colonized to Britain, then the Turkish guest workers resident in Germany, the North African migrations since the Algerian War into France, and now the flow of people into Spain and Italy. This enormous migration of peoples from south to north parallels the movements into the United States and Canada from Mexico, other parts of Latin America, and Asia, which is a movement from periphery to center that really has no precedent in history since the forced migrations and exodus from eastern Europe at the end of the nineteenth century, and before that the mass transport of millions through the slave trade in the sixteenth to eighteenth centuries.

What we are witnessing is a movement in which those from the global South—displaced by the destruction of indigenous economies, by the pricing out of crops through international and regional agreements, and by the crippling weight of debt as well as poverty, drought, and warfare pursued by the international arms trade—buy a one-way ticket and head across the borders to paradise and the American way. After all, these momentous journeys are all powered by the messages and images of the good life that we see, hear, and read daily in the global village of international communications, and which are also induced by the spread of the worldwide travel industry. These are the new global relations of power that are finally intruding the periphery into the center, eroding the symbolic boundaries between the cultural "inside" and its constitutive "outside," a process that is multiculturalizing and hybridizing the closed and homogeneous conceptions of national cultural identity, and which is, as a result, forever disturbing the delicate balance of subordinations on which their supposed purity and originary genius were constructed. The retreat of the old, core nation-states, in the face of this challenge, toward closure and defensiveness is a major fact of late twentieth-century life. The so-called culture wars, which in the United States have had a highly particular cutting edge along the racialized borders of these lines of cultural contestation, must nonetheless be now reconceptualized in terms of this wider, more historically differentiated, *global* political development. The phenomenon of the centering of the different kinds of peripheries, and thus the slow dissolution of what has stood for so long as "the West," is one of the defining features in the articulation of a variety of new kinds of modernity within our present moment.

This is not, however, a one-way development. It has its fierce other side, its negative. We have to note the vigorous efforts being made in reaction to this dilemma, the moves being made to roll back this multiculturalizing and diversifying tide—the other side to the dialectic of late modernity—which is the defensive restoration of ethnic absolutism in the struggle to cobble together new stories of cultural identity. Such developments are to be found in different forms everywhere today, in eastern as well as western Europe; in North America; in the various forms of religious fundamentalism across the globe; in the rising clamor for cultural orthodoxy in public life; and in the defense of canonical forms of knowledge, all of which are especially significant for our purposes when they cluster around a restored and transcoded variant of the nation and its narrative of national cultural identity.

In the United Kingdom we can see this in the deep suspicion of Europe that fuels the current "Little Englandism" of the anti–European Union movement, which is dead set against economic integration, the Maastricht Treaty, and everything associated with Brussels, all of which is interpreted as the loss of sovereignty for Britain. We can see another aspect of this trend in the revival of racist politics within the so-called New Europe—which is really Fortress Europe—where in Germany, France, Britain, and Italy such movements are now in alliance with the respectable right-wing political parties. We see this development further unfold in the growth of racial attacks and street violence against black and Asian people spurred on by right-wing extremism as well as in the British National Party's electoral success in Docklands and the East End of London, the very heartland of the Thatcher miracle in remaking the city as a hub for international finance. But we also see the defensive restoration of *natio* and *ethnos* in other, symptomatic moments, such as the Dewsbury school controversy in Yorkshire during the 1980s, when English children were withdrawn from primary school classes with high Muslim enrollments. We saw it too in Norman Tebbit's so-called cricket test, when the Conservative politician asked black and Asian Britons whether their loyalties lay with the English, West Indian, or Pakistani teams. Another site of contestation is in the return to canonical tradition in schemes drawn up for the teaching of literature and history, which now animates debates on Britishness in the National Curriculum in primary and secondary schools. Even in so small a sign as the culture war that is currently being fought over the issue of raising educational standards, we find the totemic mobilization in this struggle of that privileged signifier of Englishness, Shakespeare, the only dramatist who is now required to be read by all children in all schools, whether or not they can actually read at all. I do not need to underline my point here by adding to these developments the parallel debates in the United States about diversifying the canon—which has been carefully and in my view disastrously condensed by both sides into that other version of fundamentalism, "political correctness"—along with the backlash against multiculturalism now under way across schools and universities in North America as a whole, including the official version of multiculturalism in Canada as a supposedly simple matter of a pluralist mosaic.

Confronted by the openly racist turn in Germany, Italy, and France, the British are wont to be smoothly complacent. Nevertheless, the particular forms of cultural racism that have grown up in the United Kingdom under the shadow of Thatcherism have once again brought together into a single discourse questions of race, ethnicity, and cultural difference, which now condense with questions of nation, imperial decline, and cultural belonging. Here our discussion rejoins the argument I began advancing in my first lecture, for we have entered through a new turn, at a different point, into the chain of equivalences race-belonging-*ethnos*-culture-history—which I introduced there as the discourse of difference. In what has come to be called in Britain "the new racism"—for racism*s* are always historically specific, always differentiated in their effects in the different historical conjunctures in which they appear—we have a development whereby questions of cultural belonging have replaced genetic purity while functioning as a coded language for race and color, as Paul Gilroy shows in *There Ain't No Black in the Union Jack*.

You will see, in light of my previous argument, that this emphasis on cultural belonging does not silence the biological, and certainly does not eliminate the genetic-physical signifiers of racial difference and their discursive effects. Even within the language of the new racism, I would argue, the "grosser physical differences" continue to function discursively, through the metonymic sliding of the signifier, so as to fix the meaning of cultural differences beyond the contingencies of history and culture. So we now have a situation in which, even when "color" in the new variant of the discourse appears to be signifying cultural rather than biological difference, it continues silently to connote—further along the chain of equivalences—the biological-genetic signified, for which the signifier of skin color is a metonymic substitution. As I have argued, such a move is all-important, as the signified is something we cannot see. Given this qualification, I agree completely with Gilroy's observation that "a form of cultural racism which has taken a necessary distance from crude ideas of biological inferiority now seeks to present an imaginary definition of the nation as a unified *cultural* community. It constructs and defends an image of national culture, homogeneous in its whiteness yet precarious and perpetually vulnerable to attack from enemies within and without."[20]

While the British instance shows us the new face of the nation-state as a cultural broker, I do not have enough time at this point to do more than mention the related phenomenon of the resurgence of ethnic nationalism in eastern Europe. In this context, after the breakup of state socialism in 1989, we have seen a set of parallel developments often fueled by ideas of both racial purity and religious orthodoxy. The new, would-be nations of the former Soviet republics, the Baltic states, Bosnian Serbia, and elsewhere in the Balkans all paradoxically appear in the East at the very moment of the onset of relative decline among the nation-states of the West. Such developments are seeking to create new political entities in late modernity—new nation-states—as a "political roof" around supposedly homogeneous cultural identities. But since they are only able to do so in places that are actually irretrievably mixed—ethnically plural if not completely hybrid—the result of this return to closed forms of the ethnic nation is, of course, the barbarism of ethnic cleansing. On the basis of extremely dubious myths of origin, and other spurious claims that are hastily cobbled together, such ethnic nationalisms try to produce a purified "folk" that will replace the dislocated histories and hybridized ethnicities of central and eastern Europe. The aim is to advance this new, unitary cultural identity as a shield and battering ram against neighbors with whom people have peacefully dwelled for centuries. It is not clear whether this revival of ethnic nationalism is a reaction to Western modernity or a deeply confused last gasp, at one minute to midnight, of the attempt to carve out a nation from the tumbling chaos of post-Stalinist Europe as the only passport toward modernity and Western-style prosperity.

Equally disturbing, in terms of the return of particularistic nationalism and ethnic / religious absolutism (which reveals to us the dark side of the Enlightenment in the closing decades of late modernity), and equally positioned as a reactive and defensive formation to capitalist modernity, is the revival of Islamic fundamentalist movements in parts of the Middle East and Iran, but also in Algeria, Egypt, Pakistan, and elsewhere, as well as the revival of Hindu fundamentalism not only in parts of India but also across the Indian diaspora. I have deliberately insisted on appropriating the term *fundamentalism* for all these different responses to global times in late modernity, whether Eastern or Western, whether European, Asian, or Muslim, partly to resist the way in which the term has in the West come to signify the collapse of all the complex differentiations of history and political culture among Muslim and Arab societies into one grand enemy, and in part to contest the demonization of Islam as it has been mobilized by the West to substitute for the world-historical enemy it is replacing, namely, the "evil empire" of the Soviet Union as it was construed throughout the Cold War. But my use of *fundamentalism* is not merely rhetorical. I am anxious to show that what all these very different and historically specific phenomena have in common is that their response to globalization—and to the hybridization of difference that it contradictorily advances—is to reconstruct forms of cultural identity in closed, unitary, homogeneous, essentialist, and originary discursive terms. I would go so far as to say, at this level, that the distinction I made in my second lecture between the politics of difference and the politics of *différance*—that is to say, the crucial distinction between closed and open constructions of cultural identity—is one that runs right across, and completely disrupts, our conventional alignments of left/right, progressive/regressive, even racist/antiracist. What is more, I would add that disruption such as this, which bisects all of our established binary distinctions, has become, quite literally, *the* decisive political frontier of our times. It is a frontier of this kind that is at stake in the vague possibility, being tested today, as to whether a black South African could come through the barbarism of apartheid and enter into a multicultural version of "the nation" without having a conception of politics that is rooted in the difficult dialogue around difference, or whether the new South Africa will face instead the horrendous nightmare of a retreat into an ethnically cleansed, culturally unified, and homogeneous conception of the nation, which is what seems to be unfolding before our eyes in the former Yugoslavia.

"Nation," like "ethnicity," I would argue, has in itself no necessary political belongingness. Although we can think of many instances where the nation has been harnessed to regressive, archaic, and reactionary political forces—where it has been forcefully articulated to the poles of racial, ethnic, religious, and cultural closure—nationalism has also on occasion played a progressive political role, with the national liberation movements arising out of anticolonialism in Africa and Asia being a case in point. Nationalism, in this variant, has played its part in both the struggles for African decolonization and in the African American struggle against racial exclusion and oppression. But "nation" is a Janus-like phenomenon, always flashing up, like Walter Benjamin's angel of history, at a moment of danger, one face turned to the future, the other casting its hooded eyes of stone toward the past. Indeed, one of the most striking instances of the ambivalence that is ever present in the discourse of nation is the role the idea of national belongingness has played in different forms of black cultural nationalism. This was profoundly important in the 1960s struggles of African Americans and other diaspora blacks who set themselves against the dominant, often racist conception of the United States as a white nation, which was itself put into place on the basis of a closed conception of national belonging. I cannot attempt to track this complex piece of connection, and the linkages through which the idea of a "black nation" has threaded itself through the cultural politics of the black diaspora, although Paul Gilroy's *The Black Atlantic* contains some of the most significant reflections on these themes in any recent work, and is rooted in a set of profound and courageously challenging rereadings of key moments and figures in the African American canon. One of Gilroy's most important themes is the unsettling and destabilizing of the national signifier as the taken-for-granted frame in which the story of black struggles has been narrated by all sides. He substitutes for this nationalistic focus on the history of black cultural politics a new understanding of the circular interchanges, two-way traffic, cross-fertilization, and hybridization that are the driving forces for what he calls "the rhizomoporhic, fractal structure" of the black Atlantic as something that has been a transcultural formation from the start.[21]

It would be surprising indeed if a historical struggle by New World blacks to end their enslavement, win a political voice, and obtain rights and a measure of justice and equality in the national formations of the West would *not* have been drawn to the idea of an alternative political nation, to a conception of nation transformed as the guarantor of civil rights and citizenship. Similarly, it would not be surprising if diaspora blacks were drawn, if not to that alternative, then to the idea of having one's nation within a nation, or if not that, then of founding our own new nation in the place where we originally came from. All of these options in black diaspora thought concern the "nation" as the framework through which citizenship could be struggled for, secured, and guaranteed. And as Gilroy argues, in none of the key figures in the African American canon is this ever a simple matter. In very few instances does the discourse of nation persist in its basic or unmodified form, and nowhere—neither in Liberia, for instance, nor in the kingdoms of Ethiopia about which Marcus Garvey and others dreamed—has the idea of a black nation come to fruition in the form imagined or delivered by the diaspora's principal thinkers. Yet none of this destroys the power of the nation *as a discourse* and its potent effects on the black imaginary. In its most recent manifestation, the Nation of Islam has done much to capture the hearts of many disenfranchised and disillusioned young blacks, even though, under a sustained gaze, this version of the black nation does not show signs of being any more effective than the others. What is more, in terms of the closed narratives of cultural identity that the discourse of the Nation of Islam seeks to guarantee, its many costs are also now beginning to be realized.

What Gilroy's powerful rereadings also suggest is that there is another way of narrating the histories of black scattering through slavery and colonization and across the diasporas of the black Atlantic. Such rereadings can be superimposed on the grand narrative that discursively locks black people into their respective national identities, fracturing those arbitrarily imposed boundaries. This renarration cuts laterally back and forth to tell a story that is not "back to our roots" but, as Kobena Mercer puts it, "back to our routes."[22] Such a move turns on a conception of the black Atlantic as what Gilroy calls "an ex-centric, unstable, and asymmetric cultural ensemble that cannot be apprehended through the Manichean logic of binary coding." The black Atlantic is fundamentally a *transnational* way of re-reading the histories of blacks and is, by definition, a diasporic reading. For Gilroy, who has done so much in his two books to clarify the genealogies of our times, the signifier of diaspora that, he says, "was imported into Pan-African politics and black history from unacknowledged Jewish sources" disturbs the discursive economy of racial difference and cultural identity into which we have opened up an investigation, and which, he adds, offers a line of thinking that "should be cherished for its ability to pose the relationship between ethnic sameness and differentiation" as a question of "the changing same."[23]

Diasporization

It is of considerable historical, theoretical, and political importance to now follow the labyrinth so as to peer into the recessive spaces that the counterposition of the signifiers "diaspora" and "nation" opens up for cultural politics. An essential part of this genealogy is the recovery of the way in which ideas of a

Jewish diaspora fed into the discourses of African American thought and writing. This matters because it begins to undercut, and render more complex, the ways in which contemporary relations between diaspora blacks and Jews have recently hardened into a fixed antagonism which is then read back into history where it becomes mythicized, naturalized, and essentialized. Nevertheless, if you follow my discursive method of deconstruction rigorously, diaspora too has to be put under erasure before it can be put into operation for contemporary politics. One reading of diaspora, after all, is precisely that linear story of the scattering of "a chosen people" from their natal, originary homeland; the preservation of their *ethnos*—their strong sense of cultural difference—in the face of all adversity; how they held fast to their sacred texts; and how tradition was passed down through the lines of kinship and descent. What matters most to this reading are practices that produce a strong marking of "inside" and "outside," such as marriage within the group and the policing of boundaries to maintain the "purity" of tradition, all of which is crowned, in turn, by the final, sacred "return" to the promised land, which entails going back to the beginning of the story, even if that also means sitting on the heads of the people who have always shared that homeland (and indeed many of the traditions of the "chosen people") and who have gone on to make a life of their own there. In other words, it is not in my view at all impossible for a certain notion of diaspora to function discursively by suturing chains of equivalence according to a distinctively closed or fundamentalist logic, as it has done in the case of Palestine/Israel. It is only if we can unsettle these patterns, and establish an alternative chain of equivalences, that the term *diaspora* begins to function as a signifier of translation across differences, as Gilroy, Bhabha, myself, and others have been trying to make it do.

Diasporas, in my sense, are a metaphor for the discursive production of new interstitial spaces arising from the long processes of globalization in which actual physical movement and displacement are key elements of our current moment and also symptomatic of the wider consequences of global connectedness and disjuncture. The racialized diasporas characteristic of the early phases of globalization—of which slavery is the key episode—have since been compounded by a variety of other such planned and unplanned dispersals. These different histories constitute the contemporary field of proliferating antagonisms that go under the heading of "cultural difference," which is profoundly disturbing the settled self-conception of all national cultures. The challenge is to understand how these overlapping stories of diasporization must be grasped in all their similarities and differences, and how they both repeat and at the same time are dislocated from one another.

The classic scenarios of diaspora formation have been the "contact zones," as Mary Louise Pratt calls them, created by Euro-imperial expansion.[24] These primal scenes of transculturation include the plantation economies of the New World and Asia, the world's colonial cities, trading centers, and their subaltern compounds, as well as, more recently, the new, multicultural, global city. Characteristic of these primal scenes, new and old, are the complex relations of asymmetrical exchange, mutual interchange, regulated contact, and enforced exclusion among different cultures that have nonetheless irrevocably transformed the identity of everyone involved. Under the conditions of transculturation, such change never takes place on equal terms, of course, so here too we find an instance par excellence in which relations of cultural difference are also simultaneously relations of power, articulated in structures of hierarchization and subordination. Even so, such contact zones have always been the scene of cultural hybridization, creolization, and syncretism—in short, scenes of diaspora formation where different cultures not only intersect but are obliged to modify themselves in the face of one another. What situations like this call for is neither the refusal of difference nor its hardening and fixing, but its constant and ongoing negotiation.

Insofar as traditions remain relatively intact (and this is subject to enormous historical variation from one instance to another) and provided also that the conditions are propitious, the cultures of "origin"—which must be in quotation marks, for who knows whether such cultures were in fact "the same" at the beginning—will continue to exert a formative influence on what the peoples of the diaspora become, although, by definition, such origins cannot remain pure, untouched, uncorrupted, or untransformed by the other cultures with which a diaspora is obliged to interact. For similar reasons, the cultural identities that a diaspora succeeds in constructing cannot, in subsequent generations, be just a repetition of the selfsame. Diaspora cultures—convened by power and shaped by relations of symbolic and material violence—will always be inevitably syncretized, and this is what gives them their critical relevance for our global times.

In my essay about Caribbean cultural identity, I tried to put this metaphorically in terms of three imaginary presences around which such identity was constructed. There is *présence africaine,* which is the site of the repressed, of Africa's echo and trace, silenced beyond memory by the power of the experience of slavery and colonization, but still, in its trace form, a presence that is "hiding" behind every verbal and rhythmic inflection, every narrative twist and accentuation in Caribbean cultural life. There is *présence européenne,* which, by contrast, is always present, always speaking, and this is the presence into which the transported people were brutally translated and condensed, but within which we are always already inscribed, for after the break into diaspora, we are always already *in* the symbolic, *in* culture, *in* modernity—as C. L. R. James suggested, the black subject is *in* the West, even if she or he is not wholly *of* it. And then there is *présence américaine,* which is in a constant, dangerous, but never concluded dialogue with the Caribbean, as it is the presence that constitutes the very terrain of the new worlds of contact and syncretism. It is, in this sense, more "ground" than "presence," which is to say it is the site irretrievably marked in relation to the question of "origin" by an unpassable distance. It marks the "land of no return," so to speak, which is, in its own right, the beginning of diaspora, hybridity, and *différance*—all of which make the people of the Caribbean a people of diaspora, who in the United Kingdom then became twice diasporized.

I could have gone on to discuss *présence indienne,* both the indigenous Amerindians and those who migrated from South Asia, but in thinking about the co-constitutive relations of power and culture it is crucial to bear in mind that at certain strategic moments, and for certain tactical advantages of struggle, we find that one of these several "presences" is privileged over the others. The silenced can enunciate within the whole ensemble only if the settled relations of power/difference are challenged, unsettled, and recomposed. Such moves—reconfiguring the relations of power and culture as it is articulated by difference—can only be understood discursively, as I have been arguing throughout these lectures. We should never lose sight, analytically, of the fact that in such primal scenes of contact, *culture itself* has been fundamentally and irrevocably diasporized: the culture of each identity brought into the mix has been *disassembled* as a discursive structure amenable to binary closures, and—on the very ground of syncretism, hybridity, and creolization—the discourses through which identity is constructed have been *reassembled* as a structure of difference, as positionalities in a complex system of circularity and interchange, as a "weave of differences."

Here the practice of cultural politics has come, more and more, to assume the forms of what Mikhail Bakhtin describes as *heteroglossia*, the culture of many intersecting languages, the cultural politics of which creatively exploits the multiaccentuality of meaning and the carnivalesque properties of enunciation.[25] It is dialogic moves such as these that are beginning to be so culturally productive in the new diasporic spaces of our global times. As Kobena Mercer has written:

> Across a whole range of cultural forms there is a syncretic dynamic which culturally appropriates elements from the master codes of the dominant culture and "creolizes" them, disarticulating given signs and rearticulating their symbolic meaning. The subversive force of this hybridising tendency is most apparent at the level of language itself where creoles, patois,

and black English decentre, destabilize, and carnivalize the linguistic domination of English [That is, "proper," "pure," or canonical English. —S. H.]—the nation-language of master discourse—through strategic inflections, reaccentuations, and other performative moves in semantic, syntactic and lexical codes.[26]

One of the principal consequences of thinking of culture in this way is to rupture an older notion of "tradition" as the transmission, back through time, of an *un*changing same. Thus, emerging conceptions of diaspora culture break irrevocably with the closed narration of diaspora that rehearses a lament for lost authenticity, for within the traditionalist conception of diaspora culture there is always a linear movement whereby authenticity fades the further you go from its original source or depart from its sacred text, which will inevitably entail the sad declension of diaspora identity into inauthenticity and impurity. With the newer conception of diaspora, however, "tradition" is understood as itself always being remade and transformed, as something that is always *produced* as a discursive structure, thereby constantly recomposing itself as the relations of similarity and difference are repositioned—disarticulated and rearticulated—in new chains of equivalence. In breaking with the narrative of authenticity, we have a critical account of diaspora that also disrupts the fatal disposition that regards diaspora peoples as continually suspended between a traditionalism of the past, to which they cannot return—impure and corrupted as they are—and a modernity of the future, equally impure and inauthentic, which they are forbidden to enter.

The identities constructed on the basis of a diasporic conception of cultural difference are palpably not unified or unitary. They are not unified because no one dimension, no one fundamental line of difference and antagonism, can fix them or secure them once and for all time. Their being may appear to be secured in that way when it is framed within the binary racialized discourse of difference that seeks to position such identities under "race," "ethnicity" or "cultural difference" in its strong sense. Yet, as we have seen, each of these are discursive constructs that, like all worlds of meaning, can never be finally fixed, and which are open to infinite sliding among the signifiers. We must always bear in mind that other signifiers—of class, gender, and sexuality, for instance—play into and across the discourses of race, ethnicity, and cultural difference, as often as not disrupting rather than corresponding to the way identity is sutured and put into place by diasporic discourses. What results, as we can see in the cultural politics of difference in our present moment, is a multidimensional structure of similarities and differences—a "weave of differences"—which generates the contemporary politics of identity and identification as a *field of positionalities* rather than a binary structure in which positions can only repeat one another, are always in the same place, and stay fixed there until the end of time.

Diasporas are composed of cultural formations which cut across and interrupt the settled contours of race, *ethnos,* and nation. Their subjects are dispersed forever from their homelands, to which they cannot literally return. Being the product of several histories, cultures, and narratives, they belong to several homes, most of them at least in part symbolic— that is to say, imagined communities—to which there can be no return. This means that to be the subject of such diaspora is to have no one particular home to which one belongs exclusively. This is why, I suggest, diaspora subjects speak, sing, and write so eloquently in the metaphorical languages of love and loss, of memory and desire, of voyaging, travel, and return. Diasporic subjects are what Salman Rushdie calls "translated" subjects—having been carried across borders by the act of migration, those who are "translated" make a home for themselves in the interstices of the world.[27] Such subjects must learn to inhabit more than one identity, dwell in more than one culture, and speak more than one language, for as Homi Bhabha suggests, to speak in the unsettling place in between languages means to constantly negotiate and translate across their differences.[28]

Of course, such people are neither the fixed souls of the closed discourses of fundamentalism nor the vacant, wandering nomads of postmodernism or global homogenization. Diaspora subjects bear the traces of particular histories and cultures, the traditions of enunciation, the languages, texts, and worlds of meaning that have shaped them irrevocably—for with what other symbolic resources could they speak at all? But the traces at play in the formation of such identities are never singular, they are always multiple, and as such, these traces always refuse to cohere within any one single narrative of belonging. Such subjects are, it seems to me, the products of a new diasporic consciousness. These are subjects who have come to terms with the fact that in the modern world—and I believe this is true across the board—cultural identity is always *something,* but it is never just *one* thing: such identities are always open, complex, under construction, taking part in an unfinished game. As I put it elsewhere, diaspora identities "move into the future through a symbolic detour through the past. [This] produces new subjects who bear the traces of the specific discourses which not only formed them but enable them to produce themselves anew and differently."[29] The question is not *who we are* but *who we can become.* The task of theory in relation to the new cultural politics of difference is not to think as we always did, keeping the faith by trying to hold the terrain together through an act of compulsive will, but to learn to *think differently.*

NOTES

BIBLIOGRAPHY

EDITOR'S ACKNOWLEDGMENTS

INDEX

NOTES

Introduction

1. See Stuart Hall, "New Ethnicities," in *Black Film, British Cinema,* ed. Kobena Mercer, ICA Documents 7 (London: Institute of Contemporary Arts, 1988), 27–31; Stuart Hall, "Cultural Identity and Diaspora," in *Identity: Community, Culture, Difference,* ed. Jonathan Rutherford (London: Lawrence & Wishart, 1990), 222–237; David A. Bailey and Stuart Hall, eds., "Critical Decade: Black British Photography in the 80s," special issue, *Ten.8* 2, no. 3 (1992); and, Paul Gilroy, *The Black Atlantic: Modernity and Double Consciousness* (Cambridge, MA: Harvard University Press, 1993).

2. Stuart Hall, "Pluralism, Race and Class," in *Race and Class in Post-Colonial Society: A Study of Ethnic Group Relations in the English-Speaking Caribbean, Bolivia, Chile and Mexico* (Paris: UNESCO, 1978), 150–184; Stuart Hall, "Race, Articulation and

Societies Structured in Dominance," in *Sociological Theories: Race and Colonialism* (Paris: UNESCO, 1980), 305–345. See also Stuart Hall, "Gramsci's Relevance for the Study of Race and Ethnicity," *Journal of Communication Inquiry* 10, no. 2 (Summer 1986): 5–27.

3. Stuart Hall, "Reflections on 'Race, Articulation and Societies Structured in Dominance,'" in *Race Critical Theories: Text and Context,* ed. Philomena Essed and David Theo Goldberg (Malden, MA: Blackwell, 2002), 450.

4. Stuart Hall et al., *Policing the Crisis: Mugging, Law and Order, and the State* (London: Macmillan, 1978). See also Stuart Hall, "Racism and Reaction," in *Five Views of Multi-Racial Britain: Talks on Race Relations Broadcast by BBC TV* (London: Commission for Racial Equality, 1978), 23–35.

5. Stuart Hall, "Race, Culture, and Communications: Looking Backward and Forward at Cultural Studies," *Rethinking Marxism: A Journal of Economics, Culture, and Society* 5, no. 1 (Spring 1992): 10.

6. Hall's view is critically summed up in, among other texts, Stuart Hall, "The Neoliberal Revolution," *Soundings* 48 (2011): 9–28.

7. The first lecture in *The Fateful Triangle* was the basis for the lecture Hall presented at Goldsmiths College, University of London, in 1997,

which was recorded and issued as a DVD under the title *Race, the Floating Signifier* (director Sut Jhally) (Northampton, MA: Media Education Foundation, 1997); the transcript is available at www.mediaed.org/transcripts/Stuart-Hall-Race -the-Floating-Signifier-Transcript.pdf.

8. Ferdinand de Saussure, *Course in General Linguistics,* trans. Wade Baskin (London: Fontana, 1973), 120; on Saussure's conception of the sign, see Stuart Hall, "The Work of Representation," in *Representation: Cultural Representations and Signifying Practices,* ed. Stuart Hall (London: Sage, 1997), esp. 15-36.

9. See Stuart Hall, "The West and the Rest: Discourse and Power," in *Formations of Modernity,* ed. Stuart Hall and Bram Gieben, Understanding Modern Societies 1 (Cambridge: Polity, 1992), 291; see also Hall, "The Work of Representation," esp. 41-61. Limitations of the Foucauldian model are discussed in Stuart Hall, "Who Needs Identity?," in *Questions of Cultural Identity*, ed. Stuart Hall and Paul du Gay (London: Sage, 1995), 1-17.

10. Catherine Hall, "Introduction," in *Cultures of Empire: Colonizers in Britain and the Empire in the Nineteenth and Twentieth Centuries,* ed. Catherine Hall (Manchester: Manchester University Press, 2000), 17, 19.

11. W. E. B. Du Bois, *Dusk of Dawn: Toward an Autobiography of the Race Concept* (New York: Oxford University Press, 2014), 65–66. Appiah later modified his views, examining sources in German social theory that influenced Du Bois's conception of identity; see Kwame Anthony Appiah, *Lines of Descent: W. E. B. Du Bois and the Emergence of Identity* (Cambridge, MA: Harvard University Press, 2014).

12. Stuart Hall, "Minimal Selves," in *Identity: The Real Me,* ed. Lisa Appignanesi, ICA Documents 6 (London: Institute of Contemporary Arts, 1987), 45.

13. Quoted in Julie Drew, "Cultural Composition: Stuart Hall on Ethnicity and the Discursive Turn," *JAC* 18, no. 2 (1998): 184.

14. Stuart Hall, "Conclusion: The Multicultural Question," in *Un/Settled Multiculturalisms: Diasporas, Entanglements, Transruptions,* ed. Barnor Hesse (London: Zed Books, 2000), 209–241.

15. Stuart Hall, "Culture, Community, Nation," *Cultural Studies* 1, no. 3 (1993): 360.

16. On the critique of cultural studies, see Pnina Werbner and Tariq Modood, eds., *Debating Cultural Hybridity: Multi-Cultural Identities and the Politics of Anti-Racism* (London: Zed Books, 1997). Conversely, Hall's far-reaching influence on the field of transnational studies, which emerged in

the early 2000s to bridge the social sciences and humanities, is widely acknowledged; see, inter alia, Sanjeev Khagram and Peggy Levitt, eds., *The Transnational Studies Reader: Intersections and Innovations* (New York: Routledge, 2008).

17. Stuart Hall, "The *Windrush* Issue: Postscript," *Soundings* 10 (1998): 192.

18. Stuart Hall and Bill Schwarz, "Living with Difference: Stuart Hall in Conversation with Bill Schwarz," *Soundings* 27 (2007): 153, 150-151, 152.

19. Bill Schwarz, "Crossing the Seas," in *West Indian Intellectuals in Britain,* ed. Bill Schwarz (Manchester: Manchester University Press, 2003), 3.

20. *Personally Speaking: A Long Conversation with Stuart Hall*, directed by Mike Dibb (Northampton, MA: Media Education Foundation, 2009), DVD.

1. Race—The Sliding Signifier

1. W. E. B. Du Bois, "The Conservation of Races," in *W. E. B. Du Bois Speaks: Speeches and Addresses, 1890-1919,* ed. Philip S. Foner (New York: Pathfinder, 1970), 75.

2. Anthony Appiah, "The Uncompleted Argument: Du Bois and the Illusion of Race," in *"Race," Writing and Difference,* ed. Henry Louis Gates, Jr. (Chicago: University of Chicago, 1986), 21-37.

3. Du Bois, "The Conservation of Races," 75-76.

4. W. E. B. Du Bois, *Dusk of Dawn: An Essay toward an Autobiography of a Race Concept* (New York: Oxford University Press, 2014).

5. Appiah, "The Uncompleted Argument," 22.

6. Du Bois, "The Conservation of Races," 75–76.

7. Appiah, "The Uncompleted Argument," 25.

8. W. E. B. Du Bois, "Races," *The Crisis,* August 1911, 157–58.

9. Du Bois, *Dusk of Dawn,* 116–17, emphasis added.

10. Ibid.

11. Appiah, "The Uncompleted Argument," 34.

12. Crossing out a word while allowing it to remain legible is a typographic device used to designate a concept regarded as inadequate yet indispensable; see Jacques Derrida, *Of Grammatology,* trans. Gayatri C. Spivak (Baltimore: John Hopkins University Press, 1976).

13. Appiah, "The Uncompleted Argument," 34.

14. Ibid., 35.

15. Ibid., 35–36, emphasis added.

16. Ibid., 35.

17. Ibid., 22.

18. Michel Foucault introduced the concept of "regime of truth" in *Discipline and Punish: The Birth of the Prison,* trans. Alan Sheridan (London: Allen Lane, 1977), and "Truth and Power" in *Power / Knowledge: Selected Interviews and Other*

Writings, 1972–1977, ed. and trans. Colin Gordon (Brighton: Harvester), 109–133.

19. Henry Louis Gates, Jr., "Introduction," in *"Race," Writing, and Difference*, ed. Henry Louis Gates, Jr. (Chicago: University of Chicago, 1986), 5.

20. Judith Butler, *Bodies That Matter: On the Discursive Limits of "Sex"* (New York: Routledge, 1994), 11.

21. Ibid., 5.

22. Gates, "Introduction," 6; see Nancy Stepan, *The Idea of Race in Science: Great Britain, 1800–1960* (London: Macmillan, 1982).

23. Mary Louise Pratt, *Imperial Eyes: Studies in Travel Writing and Transculturation* (New York: Routledge, 1992).

24. Edmund Burke, *The Correspondence of Edmund Burke,* vol. 3, *July 1774–June 1778,* ed. George Herbert Gutteridge (Cambridge: Cambridge University Press, 1960), 351.

25. See Ernesto Laclau, "Populist Rupture and Discourse," *Screen Education* 34 (Spring 1980): 87–93; Ernesto Laclau and Chantal Mouffe, *Hegemony and Socialist Strategy: Towards a Radical Democratic Politics* (London: Verso, 1985), esp. 93–148.

26. Karl Marx and Frederick Engels, *The German Ideology,* ed. C. J. Arthur (London: Lawrence & Wishart, 1970).

27. Roland Barthes, "Myth Today," in *Mythologies,* trans. Annette Lavers (London: Jonathan Cape, 1973), 129–130.

28. Frantz Fanon, *Black Skin, White Masks,* trans. Charles Markham (New York: Grove Press, 1967), 116.

29. Ibid., 112.

30. Ibid., 109.

31. Ibid., 169.

32. Du Bois, "Races," 158.

33. Du Bois, "The Conservation of Races," 78–79.

34. Jacqueline Rose, *Sexuality in the Field of Vision* (London: Verso, 1986).

35. Sigmund Freud, "Some Psychical Consequences of the Anatomical Distinction between the Sexes," in *On Sexuality: The Pelican Freud Library,* trans. James Strachey (London: Pelican, 1977), 336.

36. Butler, *Bodies That Matter,* 8–9

37. Stuart Hall, "New Ethnicities," in *Black Film, British Cinema,* ed. Kobena Mercer, ICA Document 7 (London: Institute for Contemporary Arts, 1988), 28.

38. The concept of multiaccentuality was introduced by Mikhail Bakhtin in "Discourse in the Novel," in *The Dialogic Imagination: Four Essays,* trans. Michael Holquist (Austin: University of Texas Press, 1981), 259–422.

2. Ethnicity and Difference in Global Times

1. Anthony Appiah, "The Uncompleted Argument: Du Bois and the Illusion of Race," in *"Race," Writing and Difference,* ed. Henry Louis Gates, Jr. (Chicago: University of Chicago Press, 1986), 36.

2. Ernesto Laclau and Chantal Mouffe, *Hegemony and Socialist Strategy: Towards a Radical Democratic Politics* (London: Verso, 1985), esp. 93–148.

3. Stuart Hall, "New Ethnicities," in *Black Film, British Cinema,* ed. Kobena Mercer, ICA Document 7 (London: Institute for Contemporary Arts, 1988); see also Stuart Hall, "Ethnicity: Identity and Difference," *Radical America* 23, no. 4 (1989): 9–20.

4. See Werner Sollors, *Beyond Ethnicity: Consent and Descent in American Culture* (New York: Oxford University Press, 1986), esp. 66–101.

5. Alexis de Tocqueville, *Democracy in America and Two Essays on America,* trans. Gerald Bevan (London: Penguin 2003).

6. Werner Sollors, ed., *The Invention of Ethnicity* (New York: Oxford University Press, 1991).

7. W. E. B. Du Bois, "Of the Dawn of Freedom," in *The Souls of Black Folk* (New York: Dover, 1994), 9.

8. Bhikhu Parekh, "Superior People: The Narrowness of Liberalism from Mill to Rawls," *Times Literary Supplement,* February 25, 1994, 11–13.

9. Catherine Hall, "Missionary Stories: Gender and Ethnicity in England in the 1830s and 1840s," in *White, Male and Middle Class: Explorations in Feminism and History* (Cambridge: Polity, 1992), 204–254. The relationship between Jamaica and Britain is further examined in Catherine Hall, *Civilizing Subjects: Colony and Metropole in the English Imagination, 1830–1867* (Cambridge: Polity, 2002).

10. Jacques Derrida, "Différance," in *Margins of Philosophy,* trans. Alan Bass (Chicago: University of Chicago Press, 1984), 12.

11. See Arjun Appadurai, "Disjuncture and Difference in the Global Cultural Economy," *Public Culture* 2, no. 2 (1990): 1–24. See also Stuart Hall, "The Local and the Global: Globalization and Ethnicity," in *Culture, Globalization, and the World-System: Contemporary Conditions for the Representation of Identity,* ed. Anthony King (London: Macmillan, 1991), 19–39.

12. David Harvey, *The Condition of Postmodernity: An Enquiry into the Origins of Cultural Change* (London: Blackwell, 1991).

13. Paul Gilroy, *The Black Atlantic: Modernity and Double Consciousness* (Cambridge, MA: Harvard University Press, 1993), 199.

14. Mikhail M. Bakhtin, *The Dialogic Imagination: Four Essays,* trans. Caryl Emerson and Michael

Holquist (Austin: University of Texas Press, 1981), 425.

15. Homi Bhabha, "Of Mimicry and Man: The Ambivalence of Colonial Discourse," in *The Location of Culture* (New York: Routledge, 1994), 85–101.

16. Toni Morrison, *Beloved* (New York: Knopf, 1987).

17. Jacques Lacan, "The Mirror Stage as Formative of the Function of the 'I,'" in *Écrits: A Selection*, trans. Alan Sheridan (London: Tavistock, 1977), 1–7.

18. Edward Said, *Orientalism* (New York: Routledge, 1978), 49–73. On "landscaping" identity, see Stuart Hall, "New Cultures for Old," in *A Place in the World? Places, Cultures and Globalization*, ed. Doreen Massey and Pat Jess (Milton Keynes: Open University, 1995), 175–213.

19. Anthony Giddens, *The Consequences of Modernity* (Cambridge: Polity, 1990), 18–19.

20. Doreen Massey, "The Conceptualization of Place," in *A Place in the World? Places, Cultures and Globalization*, 58–59.

21. Doreen Massey, *Space, Place, and Gender* (Minneapolis: University of Minnesota Press, 1994), 168.

22. Stuart Hall, "The West and the Rest: Discourse and Power," in *Formations of Modernity*, ed. Stuart Hall and Bram Gieben (Cambridge: Polity, 1992), 275–331. See also Stuart Hall, "Creolization,

Diaspora and Hybridity in the Context of Globalization," in *Créolité and Creolization: Documenta 11, Platform 3,* ed. Okwui Enwezor et al. (Ostfildern-Ruit: Hatje Cantz 2003), 185-198.

23. Karl Marx and Friedrich Engels, *The Communist Manifesto,* trans. Samuel Moore (London: Penguin, 1967), 83.

24. Benedict Anderson, *Imagined Communities: Reflections on the Origins and Spread of Nationalism* (London: Verso, 1983).

25. Stuart Hall, "The Question of Cultural Identity," in *Modernity and Its Futures,* ed. Stuart Hall, David Held, and Tony McGrew (Cambridge: Polity, 1992), esp. 299-314.

26. See Mike Featherstone, ed., *Global Culture: Nationalism, Globalism, and Modernity* (London: Sage, 1990).

27. Alberto Melucci, *Nomads of the Present: Social Movements and Individual Needs in Contemporary Society,* ed. John Keane and Paul Mier (London: Hutchinson Radius, 1989).

28. Kevin Robbins, "Tradition and Translation: National Culture in Its Global Context," in *Enterprise and Heritage: Crosscurrents of National Culture,* ed. John Corner and Sylvia Harvey (London: Routledge, 1991), 21-44.

29. Although the source for this citation could not be identified, which suggests it may be Hall's

paraphrase, the ethnocentric view of precolonial societies as "outside history" is critically discussed in Claude Lévi-Strauss, "Race and History," in *The Race Question in Modern Science* (Paris: UNESCO, 1956), 123–163.

3. Nations and Diasporas

1. Cartesian conceptions of identity are discussed in Stuart Hall, "The Question of Cultural Identity," in *Modernity and Its Futures,* ed. Stuart Hall, David Held, and Tony McGrew (Oxford: Polity, 1992), 281–291; "nomads" are evoked by Gilles Deleuze and Félix Guattari, *A Thousand Plateaus: Capitalism and Schizophrenia,* trans. Brian Massumi (Minneapolis: University of Minnesota Press, 1987).

2. Mikhail Bakhtin addressed ethics in *Art and Answerability: Early Philosophical Essays,* ed. Michael Holquist and Vadim Liapunov, trans. Vadim Liapunov and Kenneth Brostrom (Austin: University of Texas Press, 1990); and in *Speech Genres and Other Late Essays,* ed. Caryl Emerson and Michael Holquist, trans. Vern McGee (Austin: University of Texas Press, 1986). The "face of the other" is discussed in Emmanuel Levinas, *Totality and Infinity: An Essay on Exteriority,* trans. Alfonso Lingis (Pittsburgh: Duquesne University Press, 1969).

3. Stuart Hall, "New Ethnicities," in *Black Film, British Cinema,* ed. Kobena Mercer, ICA Document 7 (London: Institute for Contemporary Arts, 1988), 28. Psychoanalytic approaches to identification are discussed in Stuart Hall, "Fantasy, Identity, Politics," in *Cultural Remix: Theories of Politics and the Popular,* ed. Erica Carter, James Donald, and Judith Squires (London: Lawrence & Wishart, 1995), 63–69.

4. Frantz Fanon, *Black Skin, White Masks,* trans. Charles Markham (New York: Grove Press, 1967); Frantz Fanon, *The Wretched of the Earth,* trans. Constance Harrington (London: Penguin, 1967); Frantz Fanon, *A Dying Colonialism,* trans. Haakon Chevalier (London: Penguin, 1970); Edward Said, *Orientalism* (New York: Routledge, 1978); Edward Said, *Covering Islam: How the Media and the Experts Determine How We See the Rest of the World* (New York: Routledge, 1981); Edward Said, *Culture and Imperialism* (New York: Vintage, 1993); Gayatri C. Spivak, *In Other Worlds: Essays in Cultural Politics* (London: Methuen, 1985); Sander Gilman, *Difference and Pathology: Stereotypes of Sexuality, Race and Madness* (Ithaca, NY: Cornell University Press, 1985); Homi Bhabha, *The Location of Culture* (New York: Routledge, 1994).

5. Jacques Derrida, "Différance," in *Margins of Philosophy,* trans. Alan Bass (Chicago: University of Chicago Press, 1984), 13.

6. Stuart Hall, "Cultural Identity and Diaspora," in *Identity: Community, Culture, Difference,* ed. Jonathan Rutherford (London: Lawrence & Wishart, 1990), 222–237; see Paul Gilroy, "'Sounds Authentic': Black Music, Ethnicity, and the Challenge of a 'Changing Same,'" *Black Music Research Journal* 2, no. 2 (Autumn 1991): 111–136; Paul Gilroy, *The Black Atlantic: Modernity and Double Consciousness* (Cambridge, MA: Harvard University Press, 1993), 72–110.

7. Ernest Gellner, *Nations and Nationalism,* 2nd ed. (Ithaca, NY: Cornell University Press, 2008), 6.

8. Immanuel Wallerstein, "The National and the Universal: Can There Be Such a Thing as World Culture?" in *Culture, Globalization, and the World-System: Contemporary Conditions for the Representation of Identity,* ed. Anthony King (London: Macmillan, 1991), 19.

9. Gellner, *Nations and Nationalism,* 2.

10. Bill Schwarz, "Conservatism, Nationalism and Imperialism," in *Politics and Ideology: A Reader,* ed. James Donald and Stuart Hall (Milton Keynes,UK: Open University, 1986), 106.

11. Benedict Anderson, *Imagined Communities: Reflections on the Origins and Spread of Nationalism* (London: Verso, 1983); Enoch Powell, *Freedom and Reality* (Kingswood: Elliot Right Way Books, 1969), 325.

12. Homi Bhabha, "Introduction: Narrating the Nation," in *Nations and Narration,* ed. Homi Bhabha (London: Routledge, 1990), 1.

13. Eric Hobsbawm and Terence Ranger, eds., *The Invention of Tradition* (Cambridge: Cambridge University Press, 1983).

14. See Catherine Hall, "'From Greenland's Icy Mountains . . . to Afric's Golden Sand': Ethnicity, Race and Nation in Mid-Nineteenth-Century England," *Gender and History* 5, no. 2 (Summer 1993): 212–230.

15. Timothy Brennan, "The National Longing for Form," in *Nation and Narration,* ed. Homi Bhabha (London: Routledge, 1990), 45.

16. Gellner, *Nations and Nationalism*, 45.

17. See Werner Sollors, "Introduction: After the Culture Wars; or from 'English Only' to 'English Plus,'" in *Multilingual America: Transnationalism, Ethnicity, and the Languages of American Culture,* ed. Werner Sollors (New York: New York University Press, 1998).

18. Imperialist collectivism is discussed in Stuart Hall and Bill Schwarz, "State and Society,

1880–1930," in *Crises in the British State 1880–1930,* ed. Mary Langan and Bill Schwarz (London: Hutchinson, 1982), 7–32; social imperialism is discussed in Stuart Hall, "Notes on Deconstructing 'the Popular,'" in *People's History and Socialist Theory,* ed. Raphael Samuel (London: Routledge, 1981), 227–240.

19. Catherine Hall, "White Visions, Black Lives: The Free Villages of Jamaica," *History Workshop Journal* 36 (Autumn 1993): 100–132.

20. Paul Gilroy, "The End of Anti-Racism," *New Community* 17 no 1 (October 1990): 75. See also Stuart Hall, "Racism and Reaction," in *Five Views of Multi-Racial Britain: Talks on Race Relations Broadcast by BBC TV* (London: Commission for Racial Equality, 1978), 23–35, and Martin Barker, *The New Racism: Conservatives and the Ideology of the Tribe* (London: Junction Books, 1982).

21. Gilroy, *The Black Atlantic,* 4.

22. Kobena Mercer, "Back to My Routes: A Postscript to the 80s," *Ten.8* 2, no. 3 (1992): 32–39.

23. Gilroy, *The Black Atlantic,* 198, xi. Comparative perspectives are discussed in Nicholas Mirzoeff, ed., *Diaspora and Visual Culture: Representing Africans and Jews* (New York: Routledge, 2000).

24. C. L. R. James, "Africans and Afro-Caribbeans: A Personal View," *Ten.8* 16 (1984): 55.

25. Mikhail Bakhtin, "Discourse in the Novel," in *The Dialogic Imagination: Four Essays*, ed. Michael Holquist, trans. Caryl Emerson and Michael Holquist (Austin: University of Texas, 1981) 259–422. Bakhtin's concept of the carnivalesque is addressed in Stuart Hall, "For Allon White: Metaphors of Transformation," in Allon White, *Carnival, Writing, Hysteria: Collected Essays and Autobiography* (New York: Clarendon Press, 1993), 1–25.

26. Kobena Mercer, "Diaspora Culture and the Dialogic Imagination: The Aesthetics of Black Independent Film in Britain," in *Welcome to the Jungle: New Positions in Black Cultural Studies* (New York: Routledge, 1994), 63.

27. Salman Rushdie, "Imaginary Homelands," in *Imaginary Homelands: Essays and Criticism, 1981–1991* (London: Jonathan Cape, 1991), 9–21.

28. Homi Bhabha, "How Newness Enters the World: Postmodern Space, Postcolonial Times and the Trials of Cultural Translation," in *The Location of Culture* (London: Routledge, 1994), 212–235.

29. Stuart Hall, "Culture, Community, Nation," *Cultural Studies* 7, no. 3 (October 1993): 362.

BIBLIOGRAPHY

Anderson, Benedict. *Imagined Communities: Reflections on the Origins and Spread of Nationalism.* London: Verso, 1983.

Appadurai, Arjun. "Disjuncture and Difference in the Global Cultural Economy." *Public Culture* 2, no. 2 (1990): 1–24.

Appiah, Anthony. *Cosmopolitanism: Ethics in a World of Strangers.* New York: W. W. Norton, 2006.

——. *Lines of Descent: W. E. B. Du Bois and the Emergence of Identity.* Cambridge, MA: Harvard University Press, 2014.

——. "The Uncompleted Argument: Du Bois and the Illusion of Race." In *"Race," Writing and Difference,* edited by Henry Louis Gates, Jr., 21–37. Chicago: University of Chicago Press, 1986.

Bailey, David A., and Stuart Hall, eds. "Critical Decade: Black British Photography in the 80s." Special issue, *Ten.8* 2, no. 3 (1992).

Bakhtin, Mikhail M. *Art and Answerability: Early Philosophical Essays.* Edited by Michael Holquist and Vadim Liapunov. Translated by Vadim Liapunov and Kenneth Brostrom. Austin: University of Texas Press, 1990.

———. *The Dialogic Imagination: Four Essays.* Edited by Michael Holquist. Translated by Caryl Emerson and Michael Holquist. Austin: University of Texas Press, 1981.

———. *Speech Genres and Other Late Essays.* Edited by Caryl Emerson and Michael Holquist. Translated by Vern McGee. Austin: University of Texas Press, 1986.

Barker, Martin. *The New Racism: Conservatives and the Ideology of the Tribe.* London: Junction Books, 1982.

Bhabha, Homi. "Framing Fanon." Introduction to Frantz Fanon, *The Wretched of the Earth,* vii–xli. New York: Grove Press, 2004.

———. "How Newness Enters the World: Postmodern Space, Postcolonial Times and the Trials of Cultural Translation." In *The Location of Culture,* 212–235. London: Routledge, 1994.

———. "Introduction: Narrating the Nation." In *Nations and Narration,* edited by Homi Bhabha, 1–7. London: Routledge, 1990.

———. *The Location of Culture.* London: Routledge, 1994.

———, ed. *Nation and Narration.* London: Routledge, 1990.

——. "Of Mimicry and Man: The Ambivalence of Colonial Discourse." In *The Location of Culture,* 85–101. London: Routledge, 1994.

——. "Remembering Fanon: Self, Psyche and the Colonial Condition." Introduction to Frantz Fanon, *Black Skin, White Masks,* xxi–xxxvii. London: Pluto Press, 1986.

——. "Unsatisfied: Notes on Vernacular Cosmopolitanism." In *Text and Nation: Cross-Disciplinary Essays on Cultural and National Identities,* edited by Laura García-Moreno and Peter C. Pfeiffer, 191–207. Columbia, SC: Camden House, 1996.

Braziel, Jana Evans, and Anita Mannur, eds. *Theorizing Diaspora.* Malden, MA: Blackwell, 2003.

Brennan, Timothy. "The National Longing for Form." In *Nation and Narration,* edited by Homi Bhabha, 44–70. London: Routledge, 1990.

Clifford, James. "Traveling Cultures." In *Routes: Travel and Translation in the Late 20th Century,* 17–46. Cambridge, MA: Harvard University Press, 1997.

Cohen, Robin. *Global Diasporas: An Introduction.* London: University College London Press, 1997.

Deleuze, Gilles, and Félix Guattari. *A Thousand Plateaus: Capitalism and Schizophrenia.* Translated by Brian Massumi. Minneapolis: University of Minnesota Press, 1987.

Derrida, Jacques. "Différance." In *Margins of Philosophy*. Translated by Alan Bass. Chicago: University of Chicago Press, 1984.

——. *Positions.* Translated by Alan Bass. Chicago: University of Chicago Press, 1981.

Dibb, Mike, dir. *Personally Speaking: A Long Conversation with Stuart Hall.* Northampton, MA: Media Education Foundation, 2009. DVD.

Drew, Julie. "Cultural Composition: Stuart Hall on Ethnicity and the Discursive Turn," *JAC* 18, no. 2 (January 1998): 171–196.

Du Bois, W. E. B. "The Conservation of Races." In *W. E. B. Du Bois Speaks: Speeches and Addresses, 1890–1919,* edited by Phillip S. Foner, 73–85. New York: Pathfinder, 1970.

——. *Dusk of Dawn: Toward an Autobiography of the Race Concept.* New York: Oxford University Press, 2014.

——. "Of the Dawn of Freedom." In *The Souls of Black Folk*, 9–24. New York: Dover, 1994.

——. "Races." *The Crisis,* August 1911.

Fanon, Frantz. *Black Skin, White Masks.* Translated by Charles Markham. New York: Grove Press, 1967.

——. *A Dying Colonialism.* Translated by Haakon Chevalier. London: Penguin, 1970.

——. *The Wretched of the Earth.* Translated by Constance Harrington. London: Penguin, 1967.

Featherstone, Mike, ed. *Global Culture: Nationalism, Globalism, and Modernity.* London: Sage, 1990.

Foucault, Michel. *The Archeology of Knowledge.* Translated by Alan Sheridan-Smith. London: Tavistock, 1972.

——. *Power/Knowledge: Selected Interviews and Other Writings, 1972–1977.* Edited by Colin Gordon. Brighton: Harvester, 1980.

Gates, Henry Louis, Jr., ed. *"Race," Writing and Difference.* Chicago: University of Chicago Press, 1986.

——. *Tradition and the Black Atlantic: Critical Theory in the African Diaspora.* New York: Basic Civitas, 2010.

Gellner, Ernest. *Nations and Nationalism.* 2nd ed. Ithaca, NY: Cornell University Press, 2008.

Giddens, Anthony. *The Consequences of Modernity.* Cambridge: Polity, 1990.

Gilman, Sander. *Difference and Pathology: Stereotypes of Sexuality, Race and Madness.* Ithaca, NY: Cornell University Press, 1985.

Gilroy, Paul. *The Black Atlantic: Modernity and Double Consciousness.* Cambridge, MA: Harvard University Press, 1993.

——. "Diaspora and the Detours of Identity." In *Identity and Difference,* edited by Kathryn Woodward, 299–346. London: Sage, 1997.

——. "The End of Anti-Racism." *New Community* 17 no. 1 (October 1990): 71–83.

——. *Small Acts: Thoughts on the Politics of Black Cultures.* London: Serpent's Tail, 1994.

——. "'Sounds Authentic': Black Music, Ethnicity, and the Challenge of a 'Changing Same.'" *Black Music Research Journal* 2, no. 2 (Autumn 1991): 111–136.

——. *"There Ain't No Black in the Union Jack": The Cultural Politics of Race and Nation.* London: Hutchinson, 1987.

Hall, Catherine. *Civilizing Subjects: Colony and Metropole in the English Imagination, 1830–1867.* Cambridge: Polity, 2002.

——. "'From Greenland's Icy Mountains . . . to Afric's Golden Sand': Ethnicity, Race and Nation in Mid-Nineteenth-Century England." *Gender and History* 5, no. 2 (Summer 1993): 212–230.

——. "Introduction." In *Cultures of Empire: Colonizers in Britain and the Empire in the Nineteenth and Twentieth Centuries,* edited by Catherine Hall, 1–33. Manchester: Manchester University Press, 2000.

——. "Missionary Stories: Gender and Ethnicity in England in the 1830s and 1840s." In *White, Male and Middle Class: Explorations in Feminism and History.* Cambridge: Polity, 1992.

——. *White, Male and Middle Class: Explorations in Feminism and History.* Cambridge: Polity, 1992.

——. "White Visions, Black Lives: The Free Villages of Jamaica." *History Workshop Journal* 36 (Autumn 1993): 100–132.

Hall, Stuart. *Africa Is Alive and Well and Living in the Diaspora.* Paris: UNESCO, 1975.

——. "The After-Life of Frantz Fanon: Why Fanon? Why Now? Why *Black Skin, White Masks*?" In *The Fact of Blackness: Frantz Fanon and Visual Representation,* edited by Alan Read, 12–37. London: Institute of Contemporary Arts, 1996.

——. "Aspiration and Attitude . . . Reflections on Black Britain in the Nineties." *New Formations* 33 (Spring 1998): 38–46.

——. "Black Britons." In *Social Problems of Modern Britain,* edited by Eric Butterworth and David Weir, 325–329. London: Fontana, 1972.

——. "Black Britons, Part One: Some Problems of Adjustment." *Community* 1, no. 2 (April 1970): 3–5.

——. "Black Britons, Part Two." *Community* 1, no. 3 (June 1970): 7–10.

——. "Black Diaspora Artists in Britain: Three 'Moments' in Post-war History." *History Workshop Journal* 61 (Spring 2006): 1–24.

——. "Caribbean Culture: Future Trends." *Caribbean Quarterly* 43, nos. 1–2 (March–June 1997): 25–33.

——. "Conclusion: The Multicultural Question." In *Un / Settled Multiculturalisms: Diasporas, Entanglements, Transruptions,* edited by Barnor Hesse, 209–241. London: Zed Books, 2000.

——. "Créolité and the Process of Creolization." In *Créolité and Creolization: Documenta 11, Platform 3,* edited by Okwui Enwezor et al., 27–42. Ostfildern-Ruit: Hatje Cantz, 2003.

——. "Creolization, Diaspora and Hybridity in the Context of Globalization." In *Créolité and Creolization: Documenta 11, Platform 3,* edited by Okwui Enwezor et al., 185-198. Ostfildern-Ruit: Hatje Cantz, 2003.

——. "Cosmopolitanism, Globalisation and Diaspora: In Conversation with Pnina Werbner." In *Anthropology and the New Cosmopolitanism,* edited by Pnina Werbner, 345-360. Oxford: Berg, 2008.

——. "Cosmopolitan Promises, Multicultural Realities." In *Divided Cities: The Oxford Amnesty Lectures, 2003,* edited by Richard Scholar, 20-50. Oxford: Oxford University Press, 2006.

——. "Cultural Identity and Diaspora." In *Identity: Community, Culture, Difference*, edited by Jonathan Rutherford, 222-237. London: Lawrence & Wishart, 1990.

——. "Democracy, Globalization and Difference." In *Democracy Unrealized: Documenta 11, Platform 1,* edited by Okwui Enwezor et al., 21-36. Ostfildern-Ruit: Hatje Cantz, 2001.

——. "Epilogue: Through the Prism of an Intellectual Life." In *Culture, Politics, Race, and Diaspora: The Thought of Stuart Hall,* edited by Brian Meeks, 269-291. Kingston, Jamaica: Ian Randle, 2007.

——. "Ethnicity: Identity and Difference." *Radical America* 23, no. 4 (1989): 9-20.

———. "Fantasy, Identity, Politics." In *Cultural Remix: Theories of Politics and the Popular,* edited by Erica Carter, James Donald, and Judith Squires, 63–69. London: Lawrence & Wishart, 1995.

———. "For Allon White: Metaphors of Transformation." Introduction to Allon White, *Carnival, Hysteria, and Writing: Collected Essays and Autobiography,* 1–25. Oxford: Clarendon Press, 1993.

———. "The Formation of a Diasporic Intellectual: An Interview with Stuart Hall by Kuan-Hsing Chen." In *Stuart Hall: Critical Dialogues in Cultural Studies,* edited by David Morley and Kuan-Hsing Chen, 484–503. London: Routledge, 1996.

———. "Frontlines and Backyards: The Terms of Change." In *Black British Culture and Society: A Text Reader,* edited by Kwesi Owusu, 127–130. London: Routledge, 2000.

———. "Gramsci's Relevance for the Study of Race and Ethnicity." *Journal of Communication Inquiry* 10, no. 2 (Summer 1986): 5–27.

———. "The Local and the Global: Globalization and Ethnicity." In *Culture, Globalization and the World System: Contemporary Conditions for the Representation of Identity,* edited by Anthony D. King, 19–40. London: Macmillan, 1991.

———. "Migration from the English-Speaking Caribbean to the United Kingdom, 1950–1980." In *International Migration Today,* vol. 1, *Trends and*

Prospects, edited by Reginald Appleyard, 264–310. Paris: UNESCO, 1988.

———. "Minimal Selves." In *Identity: The Real Me,* edited by Lisa Appignanesi, 44–46. ICA Documents 6. London: Institute for Contemporary Arts, 1987.

———. "The Narrative Construction of Reality: An Interview by John O'Hara." *Southern Review: Literary and Interdisciplinary Essays* 17, no. 1 (March 1984): 3–17.

———. "Negotiating Caribbean Identities (The Walter Rodney Memorial Lecture, 1993)." *New Left Review* 209 (January–February 1995): 3–14.

———. "The Neoliberal Revolution." *Soundings* 48 (2011): 9–28.

———. "New Cultures for Old." In *A Place in the World? Places, Cultures and Globalization,* edited by Doreen Massey and Pat Jess, 175–215. Milton Keynes: Open University, 1995.

———. "New Ethnicities." In *Black Film, British Cinema,* edited by Kobena Mercer, 27–31. ICA Document 7. London: Institute for Contemporary Arts, 1988.

———. "The New Europe." In *Disrupted Borders: An Intervention in Definitions of Boundaries,* edited by Sunil Gupta, 12–20. London: Rivers Oram Press, 1993.

———. "Notes on Deconstructing 'the Popular.'" In *People's History and Socialist Theory,* ed. Raphael Samuel, 227–240. London: Routledge, 1981.

———. "Old and New Identities, Old and New Ethnicities." In *Culture, Globalization and the World System: Contemporary Conditions for the Representation of Identity,* edited by Anthony D. King, 41–68. London: Macmillan, 1991.

———. "On Postmodernism and Articulation: An Interview with Stuart Hall Edited by Lawrence Grossberg." *Journal of Communication Inquiry* 10, no. 2 (Summer 1986): 45–60.

———. "Pluralism, Race and Class in Caribbean Society." In *Race and Class in Post-Colonial Society: A Study of Ethnic Group Relations in the English-Speaking Caribbean, Bolivia, Chile and Mexico,* 150–184. Paris: UNESCO, 1978.

———. "Political Belonging in a World of Multiple Identities." In *Conceiving Cosmopolitanism: Theory, Context, and Practice,* edited by Steven Vertovec and Robin Cohen, 25–31. Oxford: Oxford University Press, 2002.

———. "Politics, Contingency, Strategy: Interview with David Scott." *Small Axe: A Caribbean Journal of Criticism* 1 (March 1997): 141–159.

———. *Portrait of the Caribbean.* Six-part television series. Barraclough Carey Production for British Broadcasting Corporation and Turner Broadcasting System. New York: Ambrose Video, 1992. VHS.

———. "The Question of Cultural Identity." In *Modernity and Its Futures,* edited by Stuart Hall, David

Held, and Tony McGrew, 273–326. Oxford: Polity, 1992.

———. "Race, Articulation, and Societies Structured in Dominance." In *Sociological Theories: Race and Colonialism,* 305–345. Paris: UNESCO, 1980.

———. "Race, Culture and Communications: Looking Backward and Forward at Cultural Studies." *Rethinking Marxism: A Journal of Economics, Culture, and Society* 5, no. 1 (Spring 1992): 10–18.

———. "Racism and Reaction." In *Five Views of Multi-Racial Britain: Talks on Race Relations Broadcast by BBC TV,* 23–35. London: Commission for Racial Equality, 1978.

———. "Reconstruction Work: Images of Post-war Black Settlement." *Ten.8* 16 (1984): 2–9.

———. "Reflections on 'Race, Articulation, and Societies Structured in Dominance.'" In *Race Critical Theories: Text and Context,* edited by Philomena Essed and David Theo Goldberg, 449–454. Oxford: Blackwell, 2002.

———, ed. *Representation: Cultural Representations and Signifying Practices.* London: Sage, 1997.

———. "Stuart Hall: An Interview by Caryl Phillips." *Bomb Magazine* 58 (Winter 1997): 37–41.

———. "Subjects in History: Making Diasporic Identities." In *The House That Race Built: Black Americans, U.S. Terrain,* ed. Wahneema Lubiano, 289–300. New York: Vintage, 1998.

——. "Thinking the Diaspora: Home-Thoughts from Abroad." *Small Axe: A Caribbean Journal of Criticism* 6 (September 1999): 1–18.

——. "The West and the Rest: Discourse and Power." In *Formations of Modernity,* edited by Stuart Hall and Bram Gieben, 275–332. Understanding Modern Societies, book 1. Oxford: Polity, 1992.

——. "What Is This 'Black' in Black Popular Culture?" In *Black Popular Culture: A Project by Michele Wallace,* edited by Gina Dent, 21–36. Seattle: Bay Press, 1992.

——. "When Was the 'Post-Colonial'? Thinking at the Limit." In *The Post-Colonial Question: Common Skies, Divided Horizons,* edited by Iain Chambers and Lidia Curti, 242–260. London: Routledge, 1996.

——. "The Whites of Their Eyes: Racist Ideologies and the Media." In *Silver Linings: Some Strategies for the Eighties,* edited by George Bridges and Rosalind Brunt, 28–52. London: Lawrence & Wishart, 1981.

——. "Who Needs Identity?" In *Questions of Cultural Identity,* edited by Stuart Hall and Paul du Gay, 1–17. London: Sage, 1996.

——. "Whose Heritage? Unsettling 'the Heritage,' Re-imagining the Post-Nation." *Third Text* 49 (Winter 1999–Spring 2000): 3–13.

——. "The *Windrush* Issue: Postscript." *Soundings* 10 (Autumn 1998): 188–192.

——. "The Work of Representation." In *Representation: Cultural Representations and Signifying Practices,* edited by Stuart Hall, 13–74. London: Sage, 1997.

——. *The Young Englanders.* London: National Committee of Commonwealth Immigrants, 1967.

Hall, Stuart, Chas Critcher, Tony Jefferson, John Clarke, and Brian Roberts. *Policing the Crisis: Mugging, Law and Order, and the State.* London: Macmillan, 1978.

Hall, Stuart, and Sarat Maharaj. "Modernity and Difference." In *Modernity and Difference*, edited by Sarah Campbell and Gilane Tawadros, 36–57. Annotations, no. 6. London: Institute of International Visual Arts, 2001.

Hall, Stuart, and Bill Schwarz. "Living with Difference: Stuart Hall in Conversation with Bill Schwarz." *Soundings* 37 (Winter 2007): 148–158.

——. "State and Society, 1880–1930." In *Crises in the British State 1880–1930,* edited by Mary Langan and Bill Schwarz, 7–32. London: Hutchinson, 1982.

Hall, Stuart, and David Scott. "Hospitality's Others." In *The Unexpected Guest: Art, Writing and Thinking on Hospitality,* edited by Sally Tallant and Paul Domela, 291–304. London: Art/Books, 2012.

Harvey, David. *The Condition of Postmodernity: An Enquiry into the Origins of Cultural Change.* London: Blackwell, 1991.

Hobsbawm, Eric, and Terence Ranger, eds. *The Invention of Tradition.* Cambridge: Cambridge University Press, 1983.

Hulme, Peter. *Colonial Encounters: Europe and the Native Caribbean, 1492–1797.* London: Methuen, 1986.

James, C. L. R. "Africans and Afro-Caribbeans: A Personal View." *Ten.8* 16 (1984): 54–55.

Lacan, Jacques. "The Mirror Stage as Formative of the Function of the 'I.'" In *Écrits: A Selection,* translated by Alan Sheridan, 1–7. London: Tavistock, 1977.

Laclau, Ernesto. *New Reflections on the Revolution of Our Time.* London: Verso, 1990.

Laclau, Ernesto, and Chantal Mouffe. *Hegemony and Socialist Strategy: Towards a Radical Democratic Politics.* London: Verso, 1985.

Levinas, Emmanuel. *Totality and Infinity: An Essay on Exteriority.* Translated by Alfonso Lingis. Pittsburgh: Duquesne University Press, 1969.

Lévi-Strauss, Claude. "Race and History." In *The Race Question in Modern Science,* 123–163. Paris: UNESCO, 1956.

Marx, Karl, and Frederick Engels. *The German Ideology.* Edited by C. J. Arthur. London: Lawrence & Wishart, 1970.

Marx, Karl, and Friedrich Engels. *The Communist Manifesto.* Translated by Samuel Moore. London: Penguin, 1967.

Massey, Doreen. *Space, Place, and Gender.* Minneapolis: University of Minnesota Press, 1994.

Melucci, Alberto. *Nomads of the Present: Social Movements and Individual Needs in Contemporary Society.* Edited by John Keane and Paul Mier. London: Hutchinson Radius, 1989.

Mercer, Kobena. "Back to My Routes: A Postscript to the 80s." *Ten.8* 2, no. 3 (1992): 32–39.

——. "Diaspora Culture and the Dialogic Imagination: The Aesthetics of Black Independent Film in Britain." In *Welcome to the Jungle: New Positions in Black Cultural Studies,* 53–66. New York: Routledge, 1994.

——. *Welcome to the Jungle: New Positions in Black Cultural Studies.* New York: Routledge, 1994.

Mirzoeff, Nicholas, ed. *Diaspora and Visual Culture: Representing Africans and Jews.* New York: Routledge, 2000.

Mishra, Sudesh. *Diaspora Criticism.* Edinburgh: University of Edinburgh Press, 2007.

Morrison, Toni. *Beloved.* New York: Knopf, 1987.

Omi, Michael, and Howard Winant. *Racial Formation in the United States: From the 1960s to the 1980s.* New York: Routledge, 1986.

Papastergiadis, Nikos. *The Turbulence of Migration: Globalization, Deterritorialization and Hybridity.* Cambridge: Polity, 2000.

Parekh, Bhikhu. *Rethinking Multiculturalism: Cultural Diversity and Political Theory.* Cambridge, MA: Harvard University Press, 2000.

——. "Superior People: The Narrowness of Liberalism from Mill to Rawls." *Times Literary Supplement,* February 25, 1994.

Pieterse, Jan Nederveen. "Globalisation as Hybridisation." In *Global Modernities,* edited by Mike Featherstone, Scott Lash, and Roland Robertson, 45–68. London: Sage, 1995.

——. "Hybridity, So What? The Anti-Hybridity Backlash and the Riddles of Recognition." In *Globalization and Culture: Global Mélange,* 85–111. Lanham, MD: Rowman and Littlefield, 2004.

Powell, Enoch. *Freedom and Reality.* Kingswood: Elliot Right Way Books, 1969.

Pratt, Mary Louise. *Imperial Eyes: Travel Writing and Transculturation.* London: Routledge, 1992.

Read, Alan, ed. *The Fact of Blackness: Frantz Fanon and Visual Representation.* London: Institute of Contemporary Arts, 1995.

Robbins, Kevin. "Tradition and Translation: National Culture in Its Global Context." In *Enterprise and Heritage: Crosscurrents of National Culture,* edited by John Corner and Sylvia Harvey, 21–44. London: Routledge, 1991.

Rushdie, Salman. "Imaginary Homelands." In *Imaginary Homelands: Essays and Criticism, 1981–1991,* 9–21. London: Jonathan Cape, 1991.

Said, Edward. *Covering Islam: How the Media and the Experts Determine How We See the Rest of the World.* New York: Routledge, 1981.

———. *Culture and Imperialism.* New York: Vintage, 1993.

———. *Orientalism.* London: Penguin, 1978.

Schwarz, Bill. "Conservatism, Nationalism and Imperialism." In *Politics and Ideology: A Reader,* edited by James Donald and Stuart Hall, 154–186. Milton Keynes: Open University, 1986.

———. "Crossing the Seas." In *West Indian Intellectuals in Britain,* edited by Bill Schwarz, 1–30. Manchester: Manchester University Press, 2003.

———, ed. *West Indian Intellectuals in Britain.* Manchester: Manchester University Press, 2003.

Scott, David. "The Ethics of Stuart Hall." *Small Axe: A Caribbean Journal of Criticism* 17 (March 2005): 1–16.

Sollors, Werner. *Beyond Ethnicity: Consent and Descent in American Culture.* New York: Oxford University Press, 1986.

———. "Introduction: After the Culture Wars; or from 'English Only' to 'English Plus.'" *Multilingual America: Transnationalism, Ethnicity, and the Languages of American Culture,* edited by Werner Sollors, 1–13. New York: New York University Press, 1998.

———, ed. *The Invention of Ethnicity.* New York: Oxford University Press, 1991.

Spivak, Gayatri C. *In Other Worlds: Essays in Cultural Politics.* London: Methuen, 1985.

Taylor, Paul C. "Appiah's Uncompleted Argument: W. E. B. Du Bois and the Reality of Race." *Social Theory and Practice* 26, no. 1 (Spring 2000): 103–128.

———, ed. *The Philosophy of Race.* New York: Routledge, 2011.

Tocqueville, Alexis de. *Democracy in America and Two Essays on America.* Translated by Gerald Bevan. London: Penguin, 2003.

Wallerstein, Immanuel. "The National and the Universal: Can There Be Such a Thing as World Culture?" In *Culture, Globalization, and the World-System: Contemporary Conditions for the Representation of Identity,* edited by Anthony King, 91–106. London: Macmillan, 1991.

Werbner, Pnina, and Tariq Modood, eds. *Debating Cultural Hybridity: Multi-Cultural Identities and the Politics of Anti-Racism.* London: Zed Books, 1997.

EDITOR'S ACKNOWLEDGMENTS

I would like to express my deepest thanks to Catherine Hall and Bill Schwarz, who, as executors of Stuart Hall's literary estate, invited me to prepare *The Fateful Triangle* for publication. It has been the highest honor of my life to work with Stuart's manuscript materials. I am immensely grateful to Henry Louis Gates, Jr., director of the Hutchins Center for African and African American Research at Harvard University, and to Lindsay Waters at Harvard University Press for their role in bringing this book to publication. Over the years, countless conversations have added to my understanding of Hall's work, and I would especially like to thank John Akomfrah, Paul Gilroy, Isaac Julien, David Scott, Mark Sealy, and Gilane Tawadros for sharing their many insights. My colleagues at Yale University, past and present, have been vital to these ongoing dialogues, and alongside Hazel Carby, Michael Denning, and Caryl

Phillips, I would like to thank Elizabeth Alexander, Jacqueline Goldsby, Jonathan Holloway, Erica James, and Christopher Miller in the Department of African American Studies.

INDEX